SCIENCE
PHOTOCOPIABLES
AGES 5-7

LEVELS

1-3

- Levelled and linked to the curriculum

- Stand-alone photocopiable activities

- Ideal for mixed-age classes

Compiled by Roger Smith

CONTRIBUTORS

Text © **David Byrne**: 46, 62, 110, 111, 113, 114, 115

Text © **Frances Mackay**: 40, 41, 42, 43, 51, 52, 53, 54, 55, 56, 57, 58, 59, 84, 94, 102, 104, 105, 106, 107, 108, 109, 112, 116, 117, 118, 119, 120, 121, 122, 123, 124, 125, 126, 127

Text © **Mary Griffin**: 36, 37, 38, 39, 96, 97, 99, 100, 101

Text © **Peter Riley**: 73, 74, 76, 77, 78, 79, 80, 81, 82, 83, 86, 87, 89, 90, 91

Text © **Rob Johnsey**: 25, 33, 34, 35, 50, 92, 93, 95, 98, 103

Text © **Terry Jennings**: 15, 16, 17, 18, 19, 20, 21, 22, 23, 24, 26, 27, 28, 29, 30, 31, 32, 44, 45, 47, 48, 49, 60, 61, 63, 64, 65, 66, 67, 68, 69, 70, 71, 72, 75, 85, 88

CONSULTANT EDITOR

Roger Smith

ASSISTANT EDITOR

Wendy Tse

DESIGNERS

Lapiz Digital

COVER DESIGN

Anna Oliwa

ILLUSTRATORS

Illustration © **Maggie Brand**: 84, 94

Illustration © **Gloria**: 36, 37, 38, 39, 60, 61, 63, 64, 65, 66, 67, 68, 96, 97, 99, 100, 101

Illustration © **William Gray**: 73, 74, 76, 77, 78, 79, 80, 81, 82, 83, 86, 87, 89, 90, 91

Illustration © **Sarah Hedley**: 15, 16, 17, 18, 19, 20, 21, 22, 23, 24, 26, 27, 28, 29, 30, 31, 32, 69, 70, 71, 72, 75, 85, 88

Illustration © **Helen Herbert**: 40, 41, 42, 43, 51, 52, 53, 54, 55, 56, 57, 58, 59, 102, 104, 105, 106, 107, 108, 109, 112, 116, 117, 118, 119, 120, 121, 122, 123, 124, 125, 126, 127

Illustration © **Mike Miller**: 46, 62, 110, 111, 113, 114, 115

Illustration © **Pat Murray**: 44, 45, 47, 48, 49

Illustration © **Jenny Tulip**: 25, 33, 34, 35, 50, 92, 93, 95, 98, 103

Text and illustration copyright in individual pages as per acknowledgements. Compilation © 2006 Scholastic Ltd

Every effort has been made to trace all the copyright owners of material but there were a few cases where an author or illustrator was untraceable. Scholastic will be happy to correct any omissions in future printings.

Published by Scholastic Ltd

Villiers House
Clarendon Avenue
Leamington Spa
Warwickshire
CV32 5PR

www.scholastic.co.uk

Designed using Adobe InDesign

Printed by Bell & Bain Ltd, Glasgow

2 3 4 5 6 7 8 9   6 7 8 9 0 1 2 3 4 5

British Library Cataloguing-in-Publication Data

A catalogue record for this book is available from the British Library.

ISBN 0-439-96552-7

ISBN 978-0439-96552-1

Extracts from the Programmes of Study from The National Curriculum and the QCA Scheme of Work reproduced under the terms of HMSO Guidance Note 8 © Qualifications and Curriculum Authority.

Photocopiable pages and original teachers' notes first published in *Electricity and magnetism* (1993), *Light and colour* (1993), *Ourselves* (1993), *Paper and fabrics* (1993), *Pushing and pulling* (1993), *Seeds and seedlings* (1993), *Sound* (1993), *The Earth in space* (1993) and *Water* (1993) from the Essentials for Science series, and *Animals and plants* (1997), *Environmental Studies* (1993), *Physical processes* (1996) and *Science* (1994) from the Teacher Timesavers series.

SCHOLASTIC
www.scholastic.co.uk

NO FUSS
CONTENTS

CONTENTS

SCHOLASTIC
www.scholastic.co.uk

NO FUSS

INTRODUCTION

Science helps to provide a framework for children to develop skills and knowledge, and it is essential that children between five and seven years old observe, explore and ask questions about living things, materials and phenomena. As they are doing this they will begin to work together to collect evidence that will help them answer many simple but important scientific questions.

Some of the scientific concepts, for example forces and electricity, are difficult to understand without practical experience and science at Key Stage 1 is about practical tasks and exciting discoveries. In fact effective teaching is about finding the right task to meet the objective of the lesson and effective science teachers can draw upon a range of exciting and relevant activities. All this is made easier by young children who are naturally very curious about the world they live in and how it all works and fits together.

Each photocopiable activity is linked to the QCA Scheme of Work for Science, the Programme of Study for Science in the National Curriculum for England and the Scottish 5-14 National Guidelines, and while they don't contain everything that a busy teacher and an enthusiastic class need, they do provide a wide range of exciting material graded for the appropriate levels of attainment.

The activities are very flexible. Most can be used as stand-alone tasks and illustrate a specific objective, but they are all designed to be part of a wider series of lessons and can be used as introductory activities or can be fitted into a whole series of other lessons.

They are also flexible enough to be adapted to suit different styles of teaching. They will, for example, promote discussion; they can be used for homework; they can be given to children to plan and complete their own investigations; they can develop a scientific vocabulary and can, because some need to be completed by following teacher instructions, promote structured ways of scientific enquiry.

There are no references to Sc1 (Scientific enquiry) in the Programme of Study for Science or the 'Skills in science – investigating' section in the Scottish 5-14 National Guidelines in any of the activities. This is deliberate because it is assumed that the basic premises of collecting evidence, making observations and measurements, and trying to answer scientific questions are the key skills in learning science for young children. Teachers who are not science 'specialists' will be able to use the activities for specific lessons on light, electricity, ourselves, and so on, but at the same time they will be able to teach children to plan, ask questions, predict, follow instructions, communicate their results and make simple comparisons. Best of all, these activities will excite children and make them want to discover more and more about the complex world in which they live and the world that they will grow up to change.

Page	Activity	Objective	Teachers' notes	QCA Scheme of Work and National Curriculum links	Scottish Curriculum links	KS1 Levels
page 15	What I can do with my body	To develop vocabulary for describing the body. To identify and locate parts of the body.	It will be important to check the level of appropriate vocabulary for the class and to begin to discuss such issues as growing, moving, differences in people, and so on. Introduce the value of physical exercise to strengthen the body.	QCA Unit 1A 'Ourselves'. NC Sc2 (1) Life processes; (2) Humans and other animals; (4) Variation and classification.	Environmental Studies: Society, Science and Technology [ES] Living things and the processes of life: The processes of life – Level A	AT2 Level 1
page 16	Which side of your body do you use the most?	To observe that people differ in their preference to use their left and right hands and other body parts.	Each child needs to understand 'left' and 'right'. Ask the children to try writing with their 'wrong' hand for a few minutes, and then ask them how that feels.	QCA Unit 1A 'Ourselves'. NC Sc2 (1) Life processes; (2) Humans and other animals; (4) Variation and classification.	ES Living things and the processes of life: The processes of life – Level A	AT2 Level 1
page 17	The skeleton	To learn that humans have a skeleton of bones.	The longest individual bones are the leg bones; the shortest that the children can feel are the finger and toe bones. There are also three tiny bones inside the ear. Less able children will need support in reading some words.	QCA Unit 1A 'Ourselves'. NC Sc2 (1) Life processes; (2) Humans and other animals; (4) Variation and classification.	ES Living things and the processes of life: The processes of life – Level A/B	AT2 Level 1/2
page 18	Hair	To know that hair varies in colour, texture, thickness and strength.	This needs to be done by using several strands of long hair so it might be advisable to discuss the experiment with parents first.	QCA Unit 1A 'Ourselves'. NC Sc2 (1) Life processes; (2) Humans and other animals; (4) Variation and classification.	ES Living things and the processes of life: The processes of life – Level A	AT2 Level 1
page 19	Senses	To explore and use the five senses.	The final two questions of this activity can be developed and widened to extend each child's vocabulary and understanding of how they use their senses. You could also discuss how the senses keep us safe, for example, being able to smell if something is burning can alert us to a fire.	QCA Unit 1A 'Ourselves'. NC Sc2 (1) Life processes; (2) Humans and other animals; (4) Variation and classification.	ES Living things and the processes of life: The processes of life – Level A	AT2 Level 1
page 20	Your teeth	To identify parts of the body by close observation. To learn about cleaning teeth.	This activity involves children eating something like a biscuit – it might be advisable to let parents know what is happening and why. There are usually 20 teeth in a complete set of milk teeth, and 32 in an adult set. The milk teeth normally fall out and are replaced by adult teeth between the ages of six and twelve years. Food usually collects between the teeth and in the grooves at the tops of the back teeth. This emphasises why it is important that we brush our teeth properly.	QCA Unit 1A 'Ourselves'. NC Sc2 (1) Life processes; (2) Humans and other animals; (4) Variation and classification.	ES Living things and the processes of life: The processes of life – Level A	AT2 Level 1
page 21	Eyes	To learn about the sense of sight. To compare differences between individuals. To know that eye colour varies.	The vocabulary of this activity will need to be discussed. An extension activity could be to observe the changing size of the pupils in bright and dim light.	QCA Unit 1A 'Ourselves'. NC Sc2 (1) Life processes; (2) Humans and other animals; (4) Variation and classification.	ES Living things and the processes of life: The processes of life – Level A/B	AT2 Level 1/2
page 22	Tongues	To learn that tongue size and shape varies. To use observation to notice differences.	Tongue rolling is an inherited characteristic; it cannot be learned. The children need to know how to record their observations in a chart. To develop observation of the tongue, ask the children to consider the role of the tongue in speech.	QCA Unit 1A 'Ourselves'. NC Sc2 (1) Life processes; (2) Humans and other animals; (4) Variation and classification.	ES Living things and the processes of life: The processes of life – Level A	AT2 Level 1
page 23	Body measurements	To make comparisons about height and other body measurements.	This activity encourages children to measure accurately in centimetres. Develop this activity by measuring variation in other parts of the body, such as the head circumference.	QCA Unit 1A 'Ourselves'. NC Sc2 (1) Life processes; (2) Humans and other animals; (4) Variation and classification.	ES Living things and the processes of life: The processes of life – Level A/B	AT2 Level 1/2
page 24	All about me	To communicate observations about their qualities and differences.	When this activity is completed, the children will need time to compare their observations in pairs.	QCA Unit 1A 'Ourselves'. NC Sc2 (1) Life processes; (2) Humans and other animals; (4) Variation and classification.	ES Living things and the processes of life: The processes of life – Level A	AT2 Level 1
page 25	Watching and recording runner beans grow	To make careful observations of a plant growing.	Ensure that there is enough space available in the classroom where plants will grow well and which can be used over a period of weeks. The children can record their observations every few days, depending on the growth rate. They should observe the growth of the main and lateral roots, then the shoot, followed by the leaves.	QCA Unit 1B 'Growing plants'. NC Sc2 (3) Green plants; (5) Living things in their environment.	ES Living things and the processes of life: Interaction of living things with their environment – Level A	AT2 Level 1/2
page 26	Inside a broad bean seed	To learn what is in a seed. To recognise how plants grow.	Seeds consist of a seed coat, inside which is a food store and embryo plant. Each seed will need to be split open by an adult. Talk about why the embryo plant needs a food store.	QCA Unit 1B 'Growing plants'. NC Sc2 (3) Green plants; (5) Living things in their environment.	ES Living things and the processes of life: Interaction of living things with their environment – Level A/B	AT2 Level 1/2
page 27	Warmth and cold	To recognise that plants need warm conditions to grow successfully.	This activity requires access to a refrigerator and adequate window-sill space for several days. Talk about the differences between the conditions on a sunny window-sill and in the refrigerator. As long as the paper towels are kept moist, the seeds on the window-sill will germinate much quicker than the seeds in the refrigerator.	QCA Unit 1B 'Growing plants'. NC Sc2 (3) Green plants; (5) Living things in their environment.	ES Living things and the processes of life: Interaction of living things with their environment – Level A	AT2 Level 1/2

SCHOLASTIC
www.scholastic.co.uk

Page	Activity	Objective	Teachers' notes	QCA Scheme of Work and National Curriculum links	Scottish Curriculum links	KS1 Levels
page 28	Hairy clowns	To recognise that plants need light, moisture and warmth to grow successfully.	This activity requires access to a cupboard and window-sill space for several days. The seeds without moisture will not grow. Short, dark-green shoots should grow on the seeds on the window-sill, while the seeds in the dark cupboard will produce yellow, straggly seedlings.	QCA Unit 1B 'Growing plants'. NC Sc2 (3) Green plants; (5) Living things in their environment.	ES Living things and the processes of life: Interaction of living things with their environment – Level A	AT2 Level 1/2
page 29	Food from plants	To recognise that plants provide food for humanse can eat some parts of plants.	This activity will work even better if some real examples of fruit and vegetables are shown to the children. Talk about the different part of a plant. Parts of the plants that we can eat are: leaves – cabbages and lettuce; root – carrots and beetroot; fruit – apple, plum and grapes; seeds – peas and peanuts.	QCA Unit 1B 'Growing plants'. NC Sc2 (3) Green plants; (5) Living things in their environment.	ES Living things and the processes of life: Interaction of living things with their environment – Level A	Level 2
page 30	Fruit and vegetables	To recognise that plants provide food for humans. To understand the difference between fruit and vegetables.	It is useful to use real examples of fruit and vegetables. A fruit contains seeds; a vegetable is a leaf, stem, root, shoot or bud – it can even be a flower. The fruit on the activity sheet are: apple, orange, pear and strawberry. The others are vegetables. Carrots, potatoes and onions grow in the ground. Apples, pears and oranges grow on trees; peapods, cabbages and strawberries grow on smaller plants.	QCA Unit 1B 'Growing plants'. NC Sc2 (3) Green plants; (5) Living things in their environment.	ES Living things and the processes of life: Interaction of living things with their environment – Level A	AT2 Level 1
page 31	Which seeds do birds like best?	To recognise what seeds are. To make and record observations.	It will be useful to make several feeding platforms and to place them in different parts of the school. Birds with short, stout beaks, such as sparrows, finches and buntings, specialise in eating seeds. It is not possible to predict which seeds the birds like best, but cereal grains are often popular.	QCA Unit 1B 'Growing plants'. NC Sc2 (3) Green plants; (5) Living things in their environment.	ES Living things and the processes of life: Interaction of living things with their environment – Level A	AT2 Level 1/2
page 32	The parts of a plant	To recognise the different parts of a plant.	This is a revision activity to help children remember the vocabulary used to describe parts of a plant.	QCA Unit 1B 'Growing plants'. NC Sc2 (3) Green plants; (5) Living things in their environment.	ES Living things and the processes of life: Interaction of living things with their environment – Level A	AT2 Level 1
page 33	In the kitchen	To understand that objects can be made from different materials for different purposes.	This activity can be completed at home and it is important that the children understand the correct vocabulary for different materials. Talk about why a particular material is used for a particular object.	QCA Unit 1C 'Sorting and using materials'. NC Sc3 (1) Grouping materials.	ES Earth and space: Materials from Earth; ES Energy and forces: Forces and their effects – Level A	AT3 Level 1
page 34	In the classroom	To group materials together using a simple colour code.	The children should be encouraged to look for materials in their own classroom and to begin to develop the vocabulary of hard, soft, smooth, shiny, rough, and so on.	QCA Unit 1C 'Sorting and using materials'. NC Sc3 (1) Grouping materials.	ES Earth and space: Materials from Earth; ES Energy and forces: Forces and their effects – Level A	AT3 Level 1
page 35	Comparing materials	To recognise that materials have properties that can be explored with our senses.	Lots of other everyday materials can be displayed in the classroom and the activity can be extended to include them – but the children will need to know the necessary vocabulary.	QCA Unit 1C 'Sorting and using materials'. NC Sc3 (1) Grouping materials.	ES Earth and space: Materials from Earth; ES Energy and forces: Forces and their effects – Level A/B	AT3 Level 1/2
page 36	Packaging with paper	To understand that different kinds of paper and card are used in packaging.	A selection of paper and card packaging should be displayed in the classroom.	QCA Unit 1C 'Sorting and using materials'. NC Sc3 (1) Grouping materials.	ES Earth and space: Materials from Earth; ES Energy and forces: Forces and their effects – Level A	AT3 Level 1
page 37	Paper for mopping up spills	To suggest how to test whether materials are waterproof or absorbent.	It is important to have as wide a selection of different types of paper as possible.	QCA Unit 1C 'Sorting and using materials'. NC Sc3 (1) Grouping materials.	ES Earth and space: Materials from Earth; ES Energy and forces: Forces and their effects – Level A	AT3 Level 1/2
page 38	Which fabric keeps you warm?	To recognise that materials are chosen for specific purposes on the basis of their properties.	This activity involves using hot (but not boiling) water so there are safety issues. It would be helpful if the materials were as varied as possible. It is also possible to use a thermometer if the children can understand what measuring temperature means. Talk about the fabrics used in the type of clothes that we wear in winter.	QCA Unit 1C 'Sorting and using materials'. NC Sc3 (1) Grouping materials.	ES Earth and space: Materials from Earth; ES Energy and forces: Forces and their effects – Level A/B	AT3 Level 1/2
page 39	Keeping warm and keeping cool	To understand that materials can be sorted in different ways according to their properties.	This is a good opportunity to discuss how clothes keep us warm, cool and dry. Make a display of clothes that we wear in summer and winter. Compare the fabrics and how they feel.	QCA Unit 1C 'Sorting and using materials'. NC Sc3 (1) Grouping materials.	ES Earth and space: Materials from Earth; ES Energy and forces: Forces and their effects – Level A	AT3 Level 1
page 40	What do magnets attract?	To recognise that some materials are magnetic. To use results to draw conclusions.	The children should be encouraged to test at least ten objects and then to discuss what they have found out.	QCA Unit 1C 'Sorting and using materials'. NC Sc3 (1) Grouping materials.	ES Earth and space: Materials from Earth; ES Energy and forces: Forces and their effects – Level A/B	AT3 Level 1/2
page 41	Is it magnetic?	To predict whether an object is magnetic or not. To use results to draw conclusions saying whether their predictions were right.	All the objects need to be available in the classroom and the children should be encouraged to predict what is going to happen first. Only objects made from iron or steel are magnetic.	QCA Unit 1C 'Sorting and using materials'. NC Sc3 (1) Grouping materials.	ES Earth and space: Materials from Earth; ES Energy and forces: Forces and their effects – Level A/B	AT3 Level 1/2

SCIENCE AGES 5-7

Page	Activity	Objective	Teachers' notes	QCA Scheme of Work and National Curriculum links	Scottish Curriculum links	KS1 Levels
page 42	Will magnets work through some objects?	To explore materials and objects making and communicating observations.	All the objects need to be available in the classroom and the children should be encouraged to predict what is going to happen first. Magnetism works through non-magnetic material, but it depends on the thickness of the material, how far away the magnet is placed, and the strength of the magnet.	QCA Unit 1C 'Sorting and using materials'. NC Sc3 (1) Grouping materials.	ES Earth and space: Materials from Earth; ES Energy and forces: Forces and their effects – Level A/B	AT3 Level 1/2
page 43	Make your own magnet	To make a magnet. To make observations and communicate what happened.	The children should have access to different-sized nails. The magnet must be stroked in the same direction and lifted off the nail at the end of each stroke, not just rubbed backwards and forwards along the nail. The nail will temporarily become magnetised.	QCA Unit 1C 'Sorting and using materials'. NC Sc3 (1) Grouping materials.	ES Earth and space: Materials from Earth; ES Energy and forces: Forces and their effects – Level A/B	AT3 Level 1
page 44	Day and night	To begin to recognise that light is essential for seeing things.	It is important to use the final section of this activity as part of a whole-class lesson on sources of light. The Sun gives light during the day. We use electric lights at night, although some light comes from stars and, reflected from the Sun and the Moon. Visually impaired children will need support.	QCA Unit 1D 'Light and dark'. NC Sc4 (3) Light and sound.	ES Energy and forces: Properties and uses of energy; ES Earth and space: Earth in space – Level A	AT4 Level 1
page 45	What causes night and day?	To recognise the sun as the source of light for the Earth. To understand that day and night are caused by the Earth rotating on its axis.	Discuss the safety aspects of NEVER looking at the Sun. This activity also introduces the idea of light showing up in the dark and that there are different sources of light. Note where the United Kingdom is on the globe and rotate the globe to see when it is dawn, day, dusk and night. Visually impaired children will need support.	QCA Unit 1D 'Light and dark'. NC Sc4 (3) Light and sound.	ES Energy and forces: Properties and uses of energy; ES Earth and space: Earth in space – Level A	AT4 Level 1
page 46	Shiny and not shiny	To consider shiny and dull surfaces.	Once the objects have been correctly labelled it will be important to talk about why they are shiny – are they shiny in the dark? Light is reflected from shiny surfaces.	QCA Unit 1D 'Light and dark'. NC Sc4 (3) Light and sound.	ES Energy and forces: Properties and uses of energy; ES Earth and space: Earth in space – Level A/B	AT4 Level 1/2
page 47	Shiny things	To begin to understand the idea of reflection.	The concept of light bouncing off reflective objects could be illustrated by bouncing a torch beam off a mirror and on to a wall of a darkened room. This activity also introduces the idea of reflection related to reflective strips and safety at night. Polished metal surfaces are the shiniest, while rough or uneven surfaces are least shiny. Visually impaired children will need support.	QCA Unit 1D 'Light and dark'. NC Sc4 (3) Light and sound.	ES Energy and forces: Properties and uses of energy; ES Earth and space: Earth in space – Level A/B	AT4 Level 1/2
page 48	Shadow matching	To make observations about light shining on an object to produce a shadow. To observe that a shadow is approximately the same shape as the illuminated object that formed it.	Take the children on a walk round the school to look at both light sources and shadows. Talk about how silhouettes can be used in, for example, road signs. Visually impaired children will need support.	QCA Unit 1D 'Light and dark'. NC Sc4 (3) Light and sound.	ES Energy and forces: Properties and uses of energy; ES Earth and space: Earth in space – Level A/B	AT4 Level 1
page 49	Letting light pass through	To make observations about how light passes through some materials.	This activity can be extended by using different-coloured polythene or acetate sheets. By increasing the layers of polythene, the material will cease to be transparent; it will be translucent. If you add even more layers, it will eventually become opaque. Visually impaired children will need support.	QCA Unit 1D 'Light and dark'. NC Sc4 (3) Light and sound.	ES Energy and forces: Properties and uses of energy; ES Earth and space: Earth in space – Level A	AT4 Level 1
page 50	Making forces	To observe and describe different ways of moving.	The children should be able to identify the common forces around them. Encourage them to try all of the forces before reaching any conclusions.	QCA Unit 1E 'Pushes and pulls'. NC Sc4 (2) Forces and motion.	ES Energy and forces: Forces and their effects – Level A	AT4 Level 1
page 51	Push or pull?	To understand that pushing and pulling can make objects start or stop moving.	Extend this activity by using some practical examples of pushing and pulling.	QCA Unit 1E 'Pushes and pulls'. NC Sc4 (2) Forces and motion.	ES Energy and forces: Forces and their effects – Level A	AT4 Level 1
page 52	Pushes and pulls in the classroom	To make suggestions about how objects can be made to move.	This will be a useful activity to introduce more vocabulary about forces.	QCA Unit 1E 'Pushes and pulls'. NC Sc4 (2) Forces and motion.	ES Energy and forces: Forces and their effects – Level A	AT4 Level 1
page 53	Lifting things	To understand that there are different kinds of movement. To investigate how pulleys lift things.	The children will need to be asked a variety of questions about what heaviness means – why is a heavy bucket difficult to move? They will find it easier to lift the bucket with a pulley, but does this make a difference to how heavy the bucket is?	QCA Unit 1E 'Pushes and pulls'. NC Sc4 (2) Forces and motion.	ES Energy and forces: Forces and their effects – Level A/B	AT4 Level 1
page 54	Make it move!	To understand that objects have wheels, handles, pulleys and so on to make movement easier.	When the activity has been completed it will be useful to go through each object and suggest how it actually moves.	QCA Unit 1E 'Pushes and pulls'. NC Sc4 (2) Forces and motion.	ES Energy and forces: Forces and their effects – Level A/B	AT4 Level 1/2
page 55	Using ramps	To make suggestions about how objects can be made to move. To investigate the effect of a slope on speed and distance travelled.	The children will need to be able to measure accurately in centimetres. The greater the slope, the further the car will travel because the speed is greater. However, the greater the speed of the vehicle, the more difficult it is to stop. This activity can be extended by using different cars.	QCA Unit 1E 'Pushes and pulls'. NC Sc4 (2) Forces and motion.	ES Energy and forces: Forces and their effects – Level A/B	AT4 Level 1/2

NO FUSS

Page	Activity	Objective	Teachers' notes	QCA Scheme of Work and National Curriculum links	Scottish Curriculum links	KS1 Levels
page 56	Friction	To recognise similarities and differences in movement. To explore how friction affects the movement of objects.	The eraser will move more freely on smooth surfaces because they offer less resistance (there is less friction). This activity can be extended and as many different objects as you like can be used.	QCA Unit 1E 'Pushes and pulls'. NC Sc4 (2) Forces and motion.	ES Energy and forces: Forces and their effects – Level A/B	AT4 Level 1/2
page 57	Will it bounce?	To introduce the idea of movement up and down. To investigate factors that affect whether an object will bounce and how high it will bounce. To make predictions and reach conclusions.	When a ball hits the ground it squashes out of shape; as it springs back into shape, it pushes itself off the ground. It is important to make sure that the children predict what will happen and talk about it with their partners before they complete the activity.	QCA Unit 1E 'Pushes and pulls'. NC Sc4 (2) Forces and motion.	ES Energy and forces: Forces and their effects – Level B	AT4 Level 2
page 58	Sink or float?	To predict whether an object will float or sink. To understand that there are forces pushing against objects.	Make sure that each child predicts what is likely to happen first before carrying out the experiment. Objects that will float are the bean, the plastic ruler (if placed flat on the water), most kinds of wood and the foil tray. The wooden peg will float but the metal clip may cause it to sink. The jar may float depending on how it is placed on the water. Encourage the children to observe how they can make the jar sink or float.	QCA Unit 1E 'Pushes and pulls'. NC Sc4 (2) Forces and motion.	ES Energy and forces: Forces and their effects – Level A/B	AT4 Level 1/2
page 59	Does shape affect floating?	To understand that the shape of an object can affect the forces pushing against it.	The children may need some help in making the Plasticine shapes. The Plasticine will float if it is moulded into a shape with a large surface area.	QCA Unit 1E 'Pushes and pulls'. NC Sc4 (2) Forces and motion.	ES Energy and forces: Forces and their effects – Level A/B	AT4 Level 1/2
page 60	Everyday sounds	To understand that there are many different sources of sound and to observe sounds by listening carefully.	This activity could be done several times: in the classroom, on a walk around the school, and outside the school. Classify the sounds into those made by man-made objects and by natural objects. Hearing impaired children may need additional support.	QCA Unit 1F 'Sound and hearing'. Builds on Unit 1A 'Ourselves'. NC Sc4 (3) Light and sound; Sc2 (2) Humans and other animals.	ES Energy and forces: Properties and uses of energy – Level A/B	AT4 Level 1/2
page 61	Loud and soft sounds	To explore sounds using their sense of hearing. To understand that sounds vary in loudness and softness.	After this activity the children could identify 'loud' and 'soft' sounds around the school. Hearing impaired children may need additional support.	QCA Unit 1F 'Sound and hearing'. Builds on Unit 1A 'Ourselves'. NC Sc4 (3) Light and sound; Sc2 (2) Humans and other animals.	ES Energy and forces: Properties and uses of energy – Level A/B	AT4 Level 1/2
page 62	Which animal?	To understand that there are many different ways of making sounds.	The children might need help in identifying all the animals. Hearing impaired children may need additional support.	QCA Unit 1F 'Sound and hearing'. Builds on Unit 1A 'Ourselves'. NC Sc4 (3) Light and sound; Sc2 (2) Humans and other animals.	ES Energy and forces: Properties and uses of energy – Level A/B	AT4 Level 1/2
page 63	Sound words	To explore some of the vocabulary that describes sound.	A whole range of words that describe sounds need to be discussed and written down before completing this activity. Hearing impaired children may need additional support.	QCA Unit 1F 'Sound and hearing'. Builds on Unit 1A 'Ourselves'. NC Sc4 (3) Light and sound; Sc2 (2) Humans and other animals.	ES Energy and forces: Properties and uses of energy – Level A/B	AT4 Level 1/2
page 64	Sounds from different surfaces	To observe that the same object, dropped from the same height, makes different sounds depending on the type of surface it falls on.	It would be useful to have many more surfaces to use. Hearing impaired children may need additional support.	QCA Unit 1F 'Sound and hearing'. Builds on Unit 1A 'Ourselves'. NC Sc4 (3) Light and sound; Sc2 (2) Humans and other animals.	ES Energy and forces: Properties and uses of energy – Level A/B	AT4 Level 1/2
page 65	One ear or two?	To understand that we and other animals hear with our ears. To understand that having two ears enables us to locate the direction from which sounds are coming.	Pictures of people and animals such as elephants, bats, mice and so on would be useful to illustrate different kinds of ears. Hearing impaired children may need additional support.	QCA Unit 1F 'Sound and hearing'. Builds on Unit 1A 'Ourselves'. NC Sc4 (3) Light and sound; Sc2 (2) Humans and other animals.	ES Energy and forces: Properties and uses of energy – Level A/B	AT2 Level 1/2
page 66	Make a stethoscope	To understand that we use our sense of hearing for a range of purposes. To understand that a funnel shape picks up soft sounds and transmits them to the ear so that they can be heard more easily.	When the children have completed this activity it is useful to leave the equipment in the classroom for them to experiment with it again. Hearing impaired children may need additional support. Safety note: Do not let children put the end of the tube in their ears.	QCA Unit 1F 'Sound and hearing'. Builds on Unit 1A 'Ourselves'. NC Sc4 (3) Light and sound; Sc2 (2) Humans and other animals.	ES Energy and forces: Properties and uses of energy – Level A/B	AT2 Level 1/2
page 67	Make your own telephone	To recognise that sounds can travel through a long string.	Sounds will travel along a taut string, but not a loosely hanging string. When the children have completed this activity it is useful to leave the equipment in the classroom for them to experiment with it again. Hearing impaired children may need additional support.	QCA Unit 1F 'Sound and hearing'. Builds on Unit 1A 'Ourselves'. NC Sc4 (3) Light and sound; Sc2 (2) Humans and other animals.	ES Energy and forces: Properties and uses of energy – Level A/B	AT2 Level 1/2

Page	Activity	Objective	Teachers' notes	Scottish Curriculum links	QCA Scheme of Work and National Curriculum links	KS1 Levels
page 68	Match the sounds	To summarise some of the vocabulary that describes sound. To recognise that different animals make different sounds.	There are many more sound words that can be matched to pictures and you could make a useful matching card game to extend this activity. Hearing impaired children may need additional support.	ES Energy and forces: Properties and uses of energy – Level A/B	QCA Unit 1F 'Sound and hearing'. Builds on Unit 1A 'Ourselves'. NC Sc4 (3) Light and sound; Sc2 (2) Humans and other animals.	AT2 Level 1/2
page 69	You as a baby	To understand that animals produce young that need to be looked after. To recognise that important changes take place between babyhood and childhood.	The children will need to collect this information at home. It is important to be sensitive to those children who do not live with their birth families. A letter to parents explaining this activity might be appropriate.	ES Living things and the processes of life: The Process of life – Level A/B	QCA Unit 2A 'Health and growth'. Builds on Unit 1A 'Ourselves'. NC Sc2 (1) Life processes; (2) Humans and other animals.	AT2 Level 1/2
page 70	Growing	To understand the concept of 'growth'.	This could be used as the beginning of a whole range of practical activities measuring children in the class and in the school.	ES Living things and the processes of life: The Process of life – Level A/B	QCA Unit 2A 'Health and growth'. Builds on Unit 1A 'Ourselves'. NC Sc2 (1) Life processes; (2) Humans and other animals.	AT2 Level 1/2
page 71	Me and my friends	To make and record observations and to make simple comparisons. To recognise that people are not all the same.	The children will need to know how to measure both height and weight with the appropriate equipment.	ES Living things and the processes of life: The Process of life – Level B	QCA Unit 2A 'Health and growth'. Builds on Unit 1A 'Ourselves'. NC Sc2 (1) Life processes; (2) Humans and other animals.	AT2 Level 2
page 72	Food	To understand that we need to eat different types of food to stay healthy.	A display of different kinds of food would help the children to understand this activity better. The children could extend this investigation by making a chart of favourite foods.	ES Living things and the processes of life: The Process of life – Level A/B	QCA Unit 2A 'Health and growth'. Builds on Unit 1A 'Ourselves'. NC Sc2 (1) Life processes; (2) Humans and other animals.	AT2 Level 1/2
page 73	Types of food	To understand that we should eat lots of some food and not very much of others.	There should be lots of classroom discussion and further lessons on healthy eating. This activity can be used as part of a programme for Personal, social and health education.	ES Living things and the processes of life: The Process of life – Level A/B	QCA Unit 2A 'Health and growth'. Builds on Unit 1A 'Ourselves'. NC Sc2 (1) Life processes; (2) Humans and other animals.	AT2 Level 1/2
page 74	Using medicines	To understand that sometimes we take medicines to make us better when we are ill.	This is an interesting way of introducing the dangers of medicine and to allow children to ask questions about health and illness. Approach this topic with sensitivity if there are children who have very ill people at home or need regular medication.	ES Living things and the processes of life: The Process of life – Level B	QCA Unit 2A 'Health and growth'. Builds on Unit 1A 'Ourselves'. NC Sc2 (1) Life processes; (2) Humans and other animals.	AT2 Level 2
page 75	How good is your memory?	To observe and recall information from memory. To understand that some people are better at remembering things than others.	This is an experiment that the children should be allowed to complete in the class and then to go into older classes to see if there are differences as the children grow and get older.	ES Living things and the processes of life: The Process of life – Level B	QCA Unit 2A 'Health and growth'. Builds on Unit 1A 'Ourselves'. NC Sc2 (1) Life processes; (2) Humans and other animals.	AT2 Level 1/2
page 76	Stems and leaves	To begin to know the names of parts of plants and to use drawings to present results.	It is important that you have access to different kinds of plants near to the school. This is a good introduction to the structure of plants and illustrates that there are differences between plants. The leaves are arranged so that they each receive enough sunlight. Flowers grow from shoots that develop from a bud between the leaf stalk and stem. The correct buttercup arrangement is shown in Box C.	ES Living things and the processes of life: Variety and characteristic features; Interaction of living things with their environment – Level B	QCA Unit 2B 'Plants and animals in the local environment'. Builds on Unit 1B 'Growing plants'. NC Sc2 (3) Green plants.	AT2 Level 1/2
page 77	What the plant's parts do	To understand the differences between the parts of the plant. To understand that plants reproduce.	This activity uses wide-ranging vocabulary that needs to be discussed together along with developing the idea of reproduction in plants through seeds and fruits. The parts occur in the table in this order: I leaf, J leaf stalk, A petal, F flower stem, K main stem, C stigma, D ovule, G ovary, H seed, L root, E sepal, L root.	ES Living things and the processes of life: Variety and characteristic features; Interaction of living things with their environment – Level B/C	QCA Unit 2B 'Plants and animals in the local environment'. Builds on Unit 1B 'Growing plants'. NC Sc2 (3) Green plants.	AT2 Level 2/3
page 78	How seeds get away	To understand that seeds are spread in different ways. To make predictions.	This activity is better in the autumn when examples of different kinds of seeds can be found. Answers: 1 dandelion, ash, willow herb, sycamore; 2 tomato, gooseberry; 3 apple, date; 4 goose grass, burdock; 5 lupin, broom; 6 coconut, water-lily.	ES Living things and the processes of life: Variety and characteristic features; Interaction of living things with their environment – Level B/C	QCA Unit 2B 'Plants and animals in the local environment'. Builds on Unit 1B 'Growing plants'. NC Sc2 (3) Green plants.	AT2 Level 2/3
pages 79 & 80	Animals in the house 1 and 2	To understand that there are different kinds of plants and animals in the immediate environment.	This is a very good activity to begin a discussion about the many creatures and plants that live in our houses and gardens.	ES Living things and the processes of life: Variety and characteristic features; Interaction of living things with their environment – Level B	QCA Unit 2B 'Plants and animals in the local environment'. Builds on Unit 1A 'Ourselves'. NC Sc2 (5) Living things in their environment.	AT2 Level 2
page 81	Wildlife in a park and a pond	To understand the differences between different kinds of plants and animals found in different habitats. To begin to make a record of plants and animals found in different habitats.	You will need to link this activity with visits to a park and a pond.	ES Living things and the processes of life: Variety and characteristic features; Interaction of living things with their environment – Level B	QCA Unit 2B 'Plants and animals in the local environment'. Builds on Unit 1B 'Growing plants'. NC Sc2 (4) Variation and classification.	AT2 Level 2

NO FUSS

Page	Activity	Objective	Teachers' notes	QCA Scheme of Work and National Curriculum links	Scottish Curriculum links	KS1 Levels
page 82	Where plants live	To recognise the differences between local habitats. To recognise that different plants grow in different habitats.	This activity could be linked to a walk around the local environment to look at some of the habitats and look at what is living and growing there.	QCA Unit 2B 'Plants and animals in the local environment'. Builds on Unit 1A 'Ourselves' and Unit 1B 'Growing plants'. NC Sc2 (5) Living things in their environment.	ES Living things and the processes of life: Variety and characteristic features; Interaction of living things with their environment – Level B	AT2 Level 2
page 83	The main groups of living things	To develop an understanding that plants and animals are living things. To understand that there are similarities and differences between living things.	The main groups are: plants – algae, mosses and liverworts, ferns and horsetails, conifers, flowering plants; invertebrates (no backbone) – sponges, jellyfish, segmented worms, arthropods, molluscs, starfish; vertebrates (with backbone) – fish, amphibians, reptiles, birds and mammals. It may be useful to display a range of books that show pictures of a variety of living things.	QCA Unit 2B 'Plants and animals in the local environment'. Builds on Unit 1A 'Ourselves' and Unit 1B 'Growing plants'. NC Sc2 (4) Variation and classification.	ES Living things and the processes of life: Variety and characteristic features; Interaction of living things with their environment – Level B/C	AT2 Level 2/3
page 84	Planning a wildlife area	To develop ideas about treating animals and plants with care and respect.	Some plants need to be placed in the sun, and the pond should not be too close to lots of trees so that it does not become full of dead leaves. This could be the starting point for designing a wildlife area in your school grounds.	QCA Unit 2B 'Plants and animals in the local environment'. Builds on Unit 1A 'Ourselves' and Unit 1B 'Growing plants'. NC Sc2 (5) Living things in their environment.	ES Living things and the processes of life: Variety and characteristic features; Interaction of living things with their environment – Level B/C	AT2 Level 2/3
page 85	Living and non-living	To become aware of the wide variety of living things in the environment.	It will be necessary to list some of the characteristics of what 'living' actually means. Living things feed, move, grow, breathe, excrete (remove waste), reproduce and respond to changes.	QCA Unit 2C 'Variation'. Builds on Unit 1A 'Ourselves', Unit 1B 'Growing plants', and Unit 2B 'Plants and animals in the local environment'. NC Sc2 (1) Life processes.	ES Living things and the processes of life: Variety and characteristic features – Level B	AT2 Level 2
page 86	Signs of life	To become aware of the wide variety of living things in the environment.	This is a useful activity that reinforces the differences between living and non-living things. It is possible to show children how mould feeds and grows by displaying a piece of mouldy fruit or bread in a sealed plastic container, and observing what happens over a period of a few days.	QCA Unit 2C 'Variation'. Builds on Unit 1A 'Ourselves', Unit 1B 'Growing plants', and Unit 2B 'Plants and animals in the local environment'. NC Sc2 (1) Life processes.	ES Living things and the processes of life: Variety and characteristic features – Level B/C	AT2 Level 2/3
page 87	What do you know about humans?	To observe and recognise some simple characteristics of humans.	This activity can also be used to check what children have learned about human beings and the human life cycle. Extend this activity by discussing how people can keep healthy.	QCA Unit 2C 'Variation'. Builds on Unit 1A 'Ourselves'. NC Sc2 (1) Life processes.	ES Living things and the processes of life: Variety and characteristic features – Level B	AT2 Level 2
page 88	Measuring hands	To use simple methods to measure the area of a hand with standard units.	The hand measurements can be used to create some interesting block graphs. The next stage is to measure hand spans and create similar graphs.	QCA Unit 2C 'Variation'. Builds on Unit 1A 'Ourselves'. NC Sc2 (1) Life processes.	ES Living things and the processes of life: Variety and characteristic features – Level B/C	AT2 Level 2/3
page 89	Animals and their young	To understand that living things can be grouped according to observed characteristics. To understand that animals produce offspring and that these offspring grow into adults.	This is a useful starting point to look at a particular group of animals such as dogs, cats or birds, and to observe their characteristics more closely. Talk about how the animals will grow and observe how some young animals look like the adults, while others change dramatically.	QCA Unit 2C 'Variation'. Builds on Unit 2B 'Plants and animals in the local environment'. NC Sc2 (1) Life processes.	ES Living things and the processes of life: Variety and characteristic features – Level B	AT2 Level 2
page 90	The frog life cycle	To be aware of the variety and differences within the group of living things called animals.	This is better as a spring activity when tadpoles can be seen in the classroom and children can be taught to treat animals with care. Children should be cautioned against collecting tadpoles or going near water without adult supervision. Darwin's frog keeps its tadpoles in its throat, and the paradoxical frog has a huge tadpole and a small adult, which grows to an average of 7.6cm in length.	QCA Unit 2C 'Variation'. Builds on Unit 2B 'Plants and animals in the local environment'. NC Sc2 (1) Life processes.	ES Living things and the processes of life: Variety and characteristic features – Level B	AT2 Level 2/3
page 91	The moth life cycle	To be aware of the variety and differences within the group of living things called animals.	This activity has some difficult concepts and difficult vocabulary, both of which need to be discussed. Talk about what the children already know about moths. The largest moth is the Hercules moth.	QCA Unit 2C 'Variation'. Builds on Unit 2B 'Plants and animals in the local environment'. NC Sc2 (1) Life processes.	ES Living things and the processes of life: Variety and characteristic features – Level B/C	AT2 Level 2/3
page 92	Measuring people	To explore human variation by making observations and comparisons.	The children should know how to measure in centimetres as well as understand the meaning of some of the vocabulary such as 'circumference'. Encourage them to consider which is the most appropriate instrument when making the measurements.	QCA Unit 2C 'Variation'. Builds on Unit 1A 'Ourselves'. NC Sc2 (2) Humans and other animals.	ES Living things and the processes of life: Variety and characteristic features – Level B/C	AT2 Level 2/3
page 93	How big are your lungs?	To understand that humans are similar in some ways and different in others.	The children should understand that to conduct this experiment they need to: take in a deep breath; exhale until the bag is full; hold their breath; empty the bag; exhale again until their lungs are empty. There is always a safety issue when using plastic bags. Warn the children about the dangers of playing with polythene bags. Children with breathing difficulties should not attempt this exercise.	QCA Unit 2C 'Variation'. Builds on Unit 1A 'Ourselves'. NC Sc2 (4) Variation and classification.	ES Living things and the processes of life: Variety and characteristic features – Level B	AT2 Level 2

Page	Activity	Objective	Teachers' notes	QCA Scheme of Work and National Curriculum links	Scottish Curriculum links	KSI Levels
page 94	What are these things made from?	To begin to understand that some materials occur naturally and some do not – they are man-made.	The children could also list as many objects as possible in the classroom and try and suggest what 'natural' material they are made from.	QCA Unit 2D 'Grouping and changing materials'. Builds on Unit 1C 'Sorting and using materials'. NC Sc3 (1) Grouping materials; (2) Changing materials.	ES Earth and space: Materials from earth; Changing materials – Level B	AT3 Level 2
page 95	Making with materials	To understand that different materials are used for different purposes. To understand that many natural materials need to be treated before they are used.	Children may choose different materials for the objects depending on their experience, and some may think about objects that are made from more than one material. Many children will be very interested in how things are made and it will be fascinating to look at the progression of raw material – man-made substance – object in use: for example, oil – plastic – toy car.	QCA Unit 2D 'Grouping and changing materials'. Builds on Unit 1C 'Sorting and using materials'. NC Sc3 (1) Grouping materials; (2) Changing materials.	ES Earth and space: Materials from earth; Changing materials – Level B/C	AT3 Level 2/3
page 96	Keeping cold	To understand that some substances change when they are heated. To recognise that some materials can help to keep substances cool.	It will be useful to devise a way to record the results with the children and then to discuss what they discovered. The unwrapped ice cube should melt first as the other materials will act as insulators.	QCA Unit 2D 'Grouping and changing materials'. Builds on Unit 1C 'Sorting and using materials'. NC Sc3 (1) Grouping materials; (2) Changing materials.	ES Earth and space: Materials from earth; Changing materials – Level B	AT3 Level 2
page 97	An ice cube melting	To understand that ice is frozen water, and that it becomes water again when warmed.	The ice will melt slowly; it will change its state from solid to liquid. It is important to observe the ice at regular intervals and to discuss what happened to it and why.	QCA Unit 2D 'Grouping and changing materials'. Builds on Unit 1C 'Sorting and using materials'. NC Sc3 (1) Grouping materials; (2) Changing materials.	ES Earth and space: Materials from earth; Changing materials – Level B/C	AT3 Level 2/3
page 98	The wrong substance	To understand that different materials are used for different purposes.	This is an interesting and amusing activity. A question to ask is, What would happen if each object were really made from the wrong substance – would it work?	QCA Unit 2D 'Grouping and changing materials'. Builds on Unit 1C 'Sorting and using materials'. NC Sc3 (1) Grouping materials; (2) Changing materials.	ES Earth and space: Materials from earth; Changing materials – Level B/C	AT3 Level 2/3
page 99	What are you wearing today?	To explore everyday materials. To make observations and comparisons.	The children will need adult help in distinguishing the kind of fabric that their clothes are made from. Talk about the different kinds of natural fibres used in fabrics, such as cotton and wool. Some fibres are made from chemicals, such as nylon and polyester. Make a chart or graph to show which items of clothing are made from man-made or natural fibres or a mixture of the two.	QCA Unit 2D 'Grouping and changing materials'. Builds on Unit 1C 'Sorting and using materials'. NC Sc3 (1) Grouping materials; (2) Changing materials.	ES Earth and space: Materials from earth; Changing materials – Level B	AT3 Level 2
page 100	Types of fabrics	To recognise that fabrics are made from fibres, which are interlaced together in a number of ways. To observe that fabrics can be stretched, twisted or pulled.	Examples of items made from knitted fibres are socks and jumpers; felt is made from tangled fibres; and woven fibres are used in skirts and trousers. Use a collection of clean garments to examine these different types of fabrics. Make comparisons and sort them into sets. This activity can be extended by using many more different types of material.	QCA Unit 2D 'Grouping and changing materials'. Builds on Unit 1C 'Sorting and using materials'. NC Sc3 (1) Grouping materials; (2) Changing materials.	ES Earth and space: Materials from earth; Changing materials – Level B/C	AT3 Level 2/3
page 101	How strong are threads?	To explore the strength of different materials. To make observations and comparisons.	It is important to discuss this experiment and what the children find out about each kind of thread. Can they recognise the different types of material? The natural threads are probably not as strong as the manufactured ones, and some threads may not break at all. Examine the way the threads break, looking at where they break and what the broken ends look like. Safety note: ensure that the hook is fixed at a suitable height and it may be helpful to place a box or cushion beneath the bucket.	QCA Unit 2D 'Grouping and changing materials'. Builds on Unit 1C 'Sorting and using materials'. NC Sc3 (1) Grouping materials; (2) Changing materials.	ES Earth and space: Materials from earth; Changing materials – Level B/C	AT3 Level 2/3
page 102	Changing shapes	To understand that sometimes pushes and pulls can change the shape of an object.	Some children will introduce more 'force' words such as twist, squeeze, and stretch.	QCA Unit 2E 'Forces and movement'. Builds on Unit 1E 'Pushes and pulls' and Unit 2D 'Grouping and changing materials'. NC Sc4 (2) Forces and motion.	ES Energy and forces: Forces and their effects – Level B	AT4 Level 2
page 103	Marbles and moving air	To understand that moving air will make a force. To recognise that forces can make things speed up, slow down or change direction.	It is important to explain the difference between forces and movement: a force is needed to start or stop a movement. This activity demonstrates how a force can change the movement of a marble. It would be interesting to extend this activity by using different-sized marbles or small balls of different weights but similar sizes, such as table tennis balls and golf balls, and to see which ones are the easiest to move.	QCA Unit 2E 'Forces and movement'. Builds on Unit 1E 'Pushes and pulls' and Unit 2D 'Grouping and changing materials'. NC Sc4 (2) Forces and motion.	ES Energy and forces: Forces and their effects – Level B	AT4 Level 2

NO FUSS

Page	Activity	Objective	Teachers' notes	QCA Scheme of Work and National Curriculum links	Scottish Curriculum links	KS1 Levels
page 104	Feeling the 'push' of water	To investigate buoyancy. To say whether a prediction was correct and to try to explain the results.	Make sure that the children do predict the outcome before testing each of the weighted balls. You will need some waterproof tape and adult help for this activity. The balls will float lower in the water with each increasing weight until the combined mass is greater than the amount of water displaced, and the ball will sink.	QCA Unit 2E 'Forces and movement'. Builds on Unit 1E 'Pushes and pulls' and Unit 2D 'Grouping and changing materials'. NC Sc4 (2) Forces and motion.	ES Energy and forces: Forces and their effects – Level B/C	AT4 Level 2/3
page 105	Is salty water best for floating?	To investigate how objects float in salty and fresh water.	Children might need help in making a Plasticine shape that will hold the counters. Alternatives to plastic counters and cubes are pennies or steel washers. Salty water is more dense than tap water, so the boat will float higher and hold more counters in salty water.	QCA Unit 2E 'Forces and movement'. Builds on Unit 1E 'Pushes and pulls' and Unit 2D 'Grouping and changing materials'. NC Sc4 (2) Forces and motion.	ES Energy and forces: Forces and their effects – Level B/C	AT4 Level 2/3
page 106	Water safety	To consider which objects will float.	This is a useful 'safety' activity that can be used to introduce a longer discussion on safety near to water.	QCA Unit 2E 'Forces and movement'. Builds on Unit 1E 'Pushes and pulls' and Unit 2D 'Grouping and changing materials'. NC Sc4 (2) Forces and motion.	ES Energy and forces: Forces and their effects – Level B	AT4 Level 2
page 107	Stretch and twist	To describe ways in which the shape of objects can be changed.	It is important to have a good collection of objects that can be stretched and twisted on display in the classroom and that children can use for practical demonstrations.	QCA Unit 2E 'Forces and movement'. Builds on Unit 1E 'Pushes and pulls' and Unit 2D 'Grouping and changing materials'. NC Sc4 (2) Forces and motion.	ES Energy and forces: Forces and their effects – Level B	AT4 Level 2
page 108	Moving things	To explore how objects can be made to move faster and slower.	It is important to discuss and complete the final instruction in this activity as it summarises some of the objectives of this and earlier activities. The children should observe that rolling is easier than sliding, and that string can make pulling easier.	QCA Unit 2E 'Forces and movement'. Builds on Unit 1E 'Pushes and pulls' and Unit 2D 'Grouping and changing materials'. NC Sc4 (2) Forces and motion.	ES Energy and forces: Forces and their effects – Level B	AT4 Level 2
page 109	Rolling things	To explore how objects can be made to move faster and slower.	Ask the children to think carefully about the shapes of the objects that roll best and relate this to the use of wheels. Factors such as weight, texture and shape affect an object's ability to roll.	QCA Unit 2E 'Forces and movement'. Builds on Unit 1E 'Pushes and pulls' and Unit 2D 'Grouping and changing materials'. NC Sc4 (2) Forces and motion.	ES Energy and forces: Forces and their effects – Level B	AT4 Level 2
page 110	How do your toys move?	To use a collection of toys to illustrate how things move.	A classroom collection of toys would be useful for practical demonstrations.	QCA Unit 2E 'Forces and movement'. Builds on Unit 1E 'Pushes and pulls' and Unit 2D 'Grouping and changing materials'. NC Sc4 (2) Forces and motion.	ES Energy and forces: Forces and their effects – Level B	AT4 Level 2
page 111	Easy mover	To understand why some objects move more easily than others.	This activity introduces the concept of friction as a force that opposes movement. Try pushing these items along contrasting surfaces.	QCA Unit 2E 'Forces and movement'. Builds on Unit 1E 'Pushes and pulls' and Unit 2D 'Grouping and changing materials'. NC Sc4 (2) Forces and motion.	ES Energy and forces: Forces and their effects – Level B	AT4 Level 2
page 112	Make a buggy	To understand how to make an object move more easily.	This activity is about the best use of wheels and the importance of wheels. The holes for the axles should be at the right height to ensure that the wheels touch the ground. After allowing the children to experiment, it is important to make sure that they try using the best wheels possible on their buggies.	QCA Unit 2E 'Forces and movement'. Builds on Unit 1E 'Pushes and pulls' and Unit 2D 'Grouping and changing materials'. NC Sc4 (2) Forces and motion.	ES Energy and forces: Forces and their effects – Level B	AT4 Level 2
page 113	The great escape	To demonstrate how to make an object move slower using friction.	The discussion during and after this activity should remind children of the force of 'friction'. Different materials have different properties with regard to friction, and some materials will be better at slowing the lorry down than others. Discuss why one material may be more effective than another.	QCA Unit 2E 'Forces and movement'. Builds on Unit 1E 'Pushes and pulls' and Unit 2D 'Grouping and changing materials'. NC Sc4 (2) Forces and motion.	ES Energy and forces: Forces and their effects – Level B/C	AT4 Level 2/3
page 114	Slippery slopes	To demonstrate how a object can move more quickly by reducing friction.	Friction is lessened if the contact between two surfaces is reduced using lubricating materials. Discuss why one material may be more effective than another in making the slope more slippery. Talk about how oil can be used to reduce friction.	QCA Unit 2E 'Forces and movement'. Builds on Unit 1E 'Pushes and pulls' and Unit 2D 'Grouping and changing materials'. NC Sc4 (2) Forces and motion.	ES Energy and forces: Forces and their effects – Level B/C	AT4 Level 2/3
page 115	It's a drag!	To make measurements. To suggest how the shape of an object can affect its movement.	The addition of the card increases the vehicle's drag (or resistance), which reduces the distance travelled. This activity could be extended by using different cars and different sizes and shapes of cardboard. Discussion could also be extended by looking at streamlined designs in transport and in nature.	QCA Unit 2E 'Forces and movement'. Builds on Unit 1E 'Pushes and pulls' and Unit 2D 'Grouping and changing materials'. NC Sc4 (2) Forces and motion.	ES Energy and forces: Forces and their effects – Level B/C	AT4 Level 2/3

Page	Activity	Objective	Teachers' notes	QCA Scheme of Work and National Curriculum links	Scottish Curriculum links	KS1 Levels
page 116	Levers – 1	To investigate how levers make things easier to move.	Adult help will be required for this activity. The list of objects that use levers should be reinforced by displaying examples for the children to use. Holding the lever close to the end makes it more efficient. Safety note: take extra care with the hammer and nails.	QCA Unit 2E 'Forces and movement'. Builds on Unit 1E 'Pushes and pulls' and Unit 2D 'Grouping and changing materials'. NC Sc4 (2) Forces and motion.	ES Energy and forces: Forces and their effects – Level B/C	AT4 Level 2/3
page 117	Levers – 2	To investigate the efficiency of levers.	The lever is more efficient when the fulcrum (or pivot) is in the middle and the pushing force is applied at a distance from the fulcrum. Less effort is needed if the fulcrum is placed closer to the end where the pushing force is applied. It is important to allow the children to discuss the results of this activity and to try to use their 'forces' vocabulary to explain what happened.	QCA Unit 2E 'Forces and movement'. Builds on Unit 1E 'Pushes and pulls' and Unit 2D 'Grouping and changing materials'. NC Sc4 (2) Forces and motion.	ES Energy and forces: Forces and their effects – Level B/C	AT4 Level 2/3
page 118	See-saw	To understand that it is possible to balance forces.	The coins balance because the centre of gravity is in the middle. This activity could be extended by using balances or using as part of a maths activity. Work = force x distance, so two coins placed 2cm from the fulcrum (2 x 2 = 4) will balance one coin placed 4cm from the fulcrum (1 x 4 = 4).	QCA Unit 2E 'Forces and movement'. Builds on Unit 1E 'Pushes and pulls' and Unit 2D 'Grouping and changing materials'. NC Sc4 (2) Forces and motion.	ES Energy and forces: Forces and their effects – Level B	AT4 Level 2
page 119	Make a puppet	To understand that a force in one direction can make things move in a different one.	This is a long activity that needs to take place over a period of days and will need adult help and supervision.	QCA Unit 2E 'Forces and movement'. Builds on Unit 1E 'Pushes and pulls' and Unit 2D 'Grouping and changing materials'. NC Sc4 (2) Forces and motion.	ES Energy and forces: Forces and their effects – Level B/C	AT4 Level 2/3
page 120	Where is electricity?	To recognise that everyday appliances use electricity and that electricity can come from the mains or battery.	This activity could be extended to look at electricity in the classroom, in the school, and at home.	QCA Unit 2F 'Using electricity'. Builds on Unit 1C 'Sorting and using materials' and Unit 1D 'Light and dark'. NC Sc4 (1) Electricity.	ES Energy and forces: Properties and uses of energy – Level B	AT4 Level 2
page 121	Which of these objects use electricity?	To recognise that electricity [from battery and the mains] causes things to move, light up, heat up and make sounds.	It would be helpful to have examples in the classroom so that the uses of electricity can be demonstrated to the children.	QCA Unit 2F 'Using electricity'. Builds on Unit 1C 'Sorting and using materials' and Unit 1D 'Light and dark'. NC Sc4 (1) Electricity.	ES Energy and forces: Properties and uses of energy – Level B	AT4 Level 2
page 122	What is unsafe here?	To recognise that everyday appliances are connected to the mains and must be used safely.	Many more examples could be used so that children really understand how dangerous electricity can be.	QCA Unit 2F 'Using electricity'. Builds on Unit 1C 'Sorting and using materials' and Unit 1D 'Light and dark'. NC Sc4 (1) Electricity.	ES Energy and forces: Properties and uses of energy – Level B	AT4 Level 2
page 123	Make a bulb light up	To make a complete circuit using battery, wires and bulbs.	The vocabulary of electricity should be introduced to the children: for example, bulb, battery, socket, plug, bulb holder and wire. It is important to make a complete circuit. Attach wires to both ends of the battery and ensure that they are screwed in on both sides of the bulb holder. Electricity flows in one direction so check that the arrows go round the circuit in the same direction. Don't forget to check that all the pieces of equipment are in working order.	QCA Unit 2F 'Using electricity'. Builds on Unit 1C 'Sorting and using materials' and Unit 1D 'Light and dark'. NC Sc4 (1) Electricity.	ES Energy and forces: Properties and uses of energy – Level B/C	AT4 Level 2/3
page 124	Which bulb will light up?	To explain how to make a bulb light up and what happens.	Explain to the children that they must predict what will happen before they try to connect the bulb, battery and wires. Only arrangement 5 will light up: the wires must touch both ends of the battery and both sides of the bulb's metal base.	QCA Unit 2F 'Using electricity'. Builds on Unit 1C 'Sorting and using materials' and Unit 1D 'Light and dark'. NC Sc4 (1) Electricity.	ES Energy and forces: Properties and uses of energy – Level B/C	AT4 Level 2/3
page 125	Make a simple switch	To understand that an electrical device will not work if there is a break in the circuit.	Discuss with the children how a switch works and what causes the bulb to go on or off. A complete circuit is necessary for the bulb to light up. Ensure that the paper fasteners on the switch do not touch each other underneath the card because the circuit will not be complete if they do.	QCA Unit 2F 'Using electricity'. Builds on Unit 1C 'Sorting and using materials' and Unit 1D 'Light and dark'. NC Sc4 (1) Electricity.	ES Energy and forces: Properties and uses of energy – Level B/C	AT4 Level 2/3
page 126	Make it buzz!	To use circuits to make simple devices.	The buzzer will only work one way so the children will need to experiment to find the correct direction. This illustrates how electricity flows in one direction in a circuit. This activity will need adult help and could be linked to work on design and technology.	QCA Unit 2F 'Using electricity'. Builds on Unit 1C 'Sorting and using materials' and Unit 1D 'Light and dark'. NC Sc4 (1) Electricity.	ES Energy and forces: Properties and uses of energy – Level B/C	AT4 Level 2/3
page 127	Will it conduct electricity?	To make and test predictions about circuits. To record observations.	The children have to know how to make a simple circuit that works properly before they start this activity. Only the metal objects will conduct electricity. This activity will emphasise the importance of a complete circuit with good connections.	QCA Unit 2F 'Using electricity'. Builds on Unit 1C 'Sorting and using materials' and Unit 1D 'Light and dark'. NC Sc4 (1) Electricity.	ES Energy and forces: Properties and uses of energy – Level B/C	AT4 Level 2/3

SCHOLASTIC
www.scholastic.co.uk

What I can do with my body

You will need: a pencil.

▲ Look at these pictures. Say which part of your body you use for each of these activities. Choose from: hands, legs, head, eyes, ears and your whole body.

Which side of your body do you use the most?

You will need: a pen.

▲ Are you left-handed or right-handed? Pick up a pen and see.

▲ Scratch your back. Which hand do you use?

▲ Cup your hand to hear better. Which ear do you use?

▲ Wink at someone. Which eye do you use?

▲ Tilt your head on your shoulder. Which shoulder does your head touch?

SCHOLASTIC
www.scholastic.co.uk

Name _____

The skeleton

You will need: a tape measure.

▲ Look at this picture of a skeleton. It is made up of bones.
▲ Can you feel your bones?
▲ Measure some of your bones.

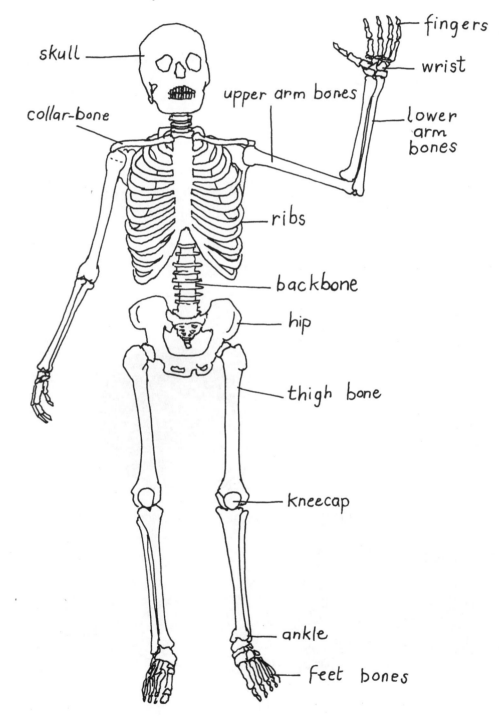

▲ Which is the longest bone you can find? Which is
the shortest?

NO FUSS
PHOTOCOPIABLE

Hair

You will need: a long hair; sticky tape; paper; paper-clips; a pencil.

▲ What colour is your hair? Is it brown, black, red or fair?

My hair is _____

▲ How strong is a hair? Fix a long hair like in the picture below with a paper loop on the end. Put paper-clips, one at a time, into the loop of paper attached to the hair.

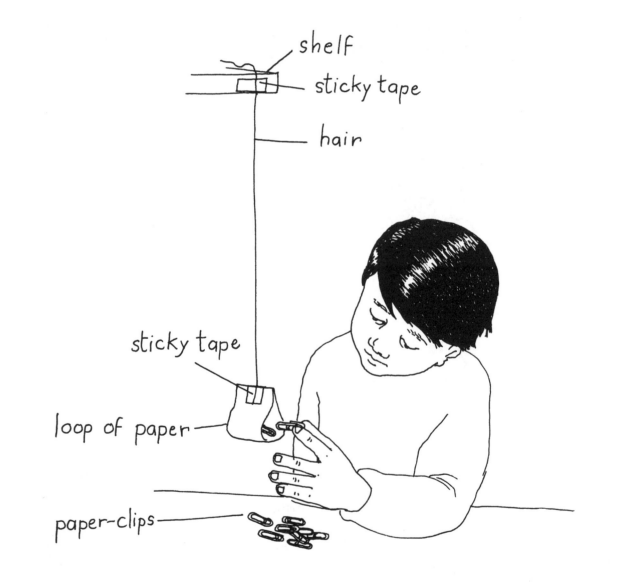

▲ Try this again with a hair from someone else.

Name _____

Senses

You will need: a pencil; a ruler.

▲ You have five senses. Match the sentence with the right part of the body.

• You see with your

• You hear with your

• You smell with your

• You touch with your

• You taste with your

▲ Which sense do you use most?

▲ Which senses do you use when eating your food?

Name _____

Your teeth

You will need: a small mirror; a chocolate biscuit; coloured pencils; a pencil.

▲ Look in the mirror at your teeth. Colour the tooth chart to show your teeth. How many teeth do you have altogether?

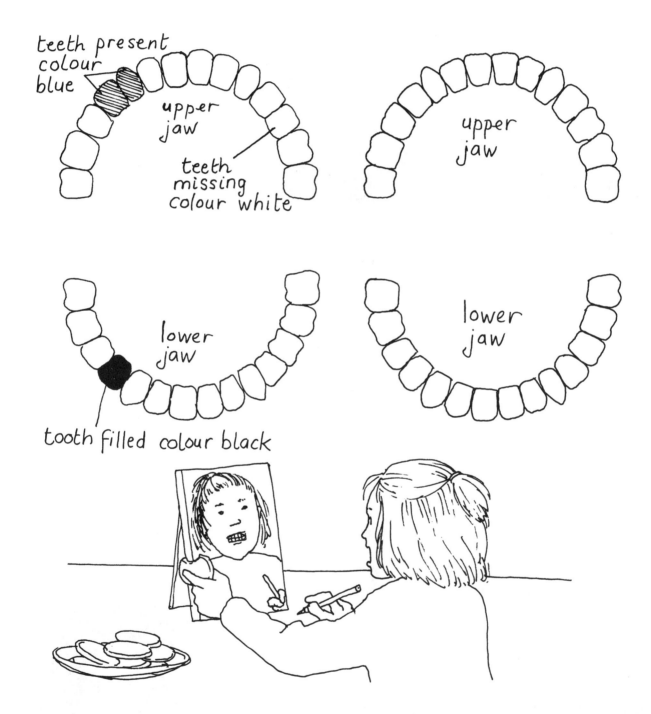

▲ Chew the chocolate biscuit and look in the mirror. Where does the chocolate collect? Show these places on your chart.
▲ Why should we clean our teeth after meals?

Eyes

You will need: a mirror; a pencil.

▲ Look in the mirror. Look at your eyes.

Can you see the parts shown in the picture?

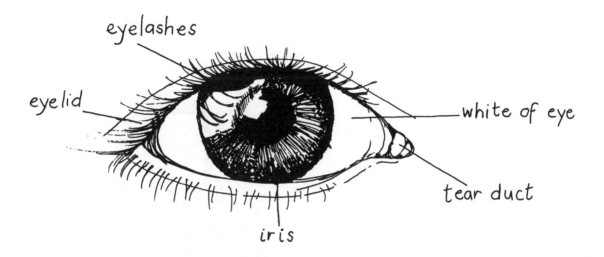

 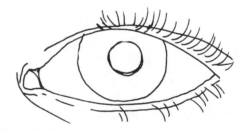

▲ Colour the picture.

▲ Are your friends' eyes the same colour as yours?

Tongues

You will need: a mirror; a pencil.

▲ Is everyone's tongue the same? Look in the mirror.
Is your tongue round or pointed?

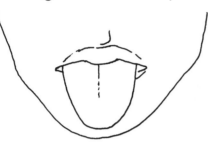

▲ Can you touch your nose with your tongue?

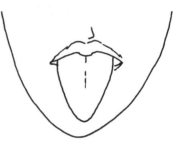

▲ Can you roll your tongue like this?

▲ Make a chart like this.
Say what your tongue and your friends' tongues are like.

Name	Round or pointed	Can roll tongue	Can touch nose with tongue

SCHOLASTIC
www.scholastic.co.uk

Name _____

Body measurements

You will need: a tape measure; a pencil.

Work with a friend.

▲ Measure how tall you are.　　　I am _____ cm high.

▲ Measure your hand-span.　　　My hand-span is _____ cm.

▲ Measure your foot.　　　My foot is _____ cm long.

▲ Measure your arm-span.　　　My arm-span is _____ cm.

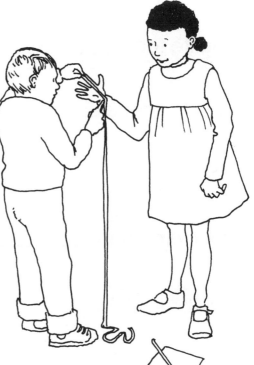

▲ Now measure your friend. Are your friend's measurements the same as yours?

All about me

You will need: a pencil; glue; scissors; paper.

▲ Make a book about yourself. Call it 'All about Me'.
Stick some pictures of yourself in it. Put your fingerprints,
handprints and footprints in it. Write down this information
about yourself.

My height _____ My weight _____

The colour of my eyes _____ The colour of my hair _____

My favourite food _____ My favourite drink _____

My favourite animal _____ My favourite sport _____

My favourite television programme _____

My favourite colour _____

My favourite singer _____

▲ Compare your book with those of your friends.
Is there anyone else exactly like you?

Watching and recording runner beans grow

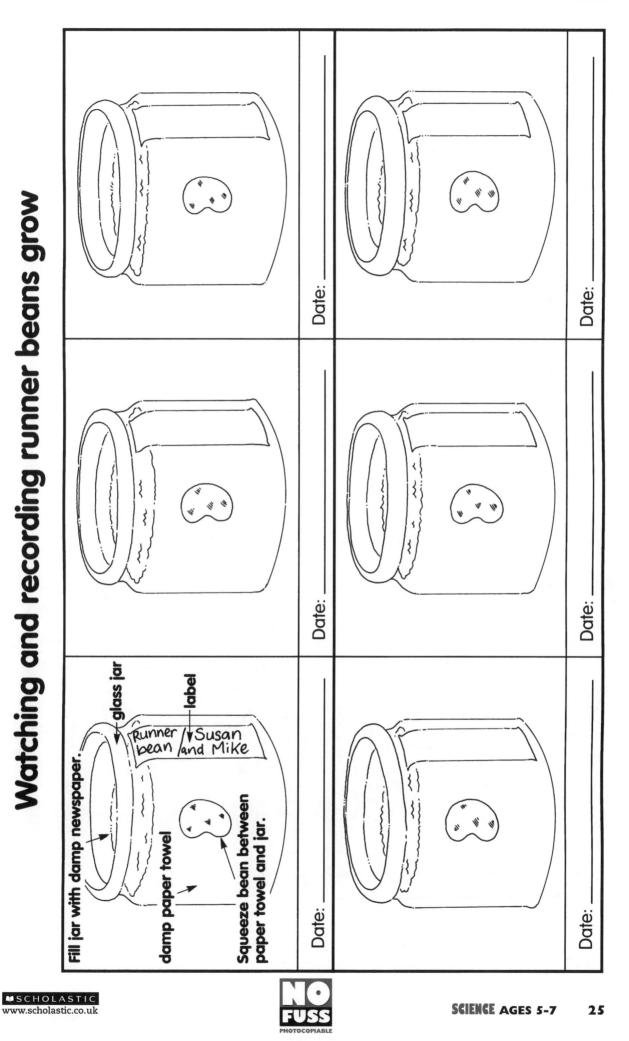

glass jar

label

Runner bean → Susan and Mike

Fill jar with damp newspaper.

damp paper towel

Squeeze bean between paper towel and jar.

Date: _____

Date: _____

Date: _____

Date: _____

Date: _____

Name _____

Inside a broad bean seed

You will need: a dish of cold water; a broad bean seed; a hand lens; a pencil.

▲ Soak a broad bean seed in cold water overnight.

▲ The next day, carefully split the seed open.

▲ Look at the inside of the bean with a hand lens.

Can you see a tiny plant? It is called an embryo.

Can you see a food store? The tiny plant uses this food when it grows.

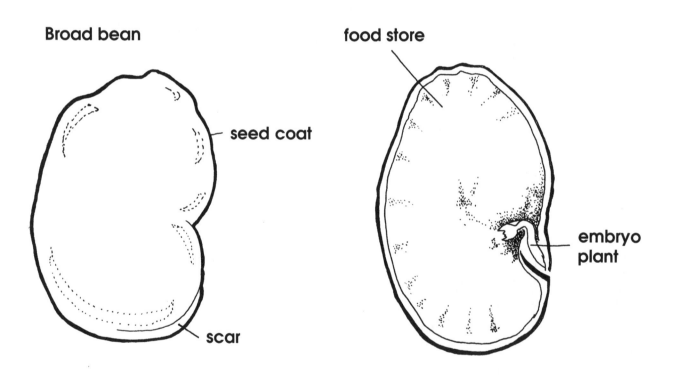

Broad bean

seed coat

scar

food store

embryo plant

▲ Now look at the insides of other seeds.

Do they all have an embryo?

Do they all have a food store?

Warmth and cold

You will need: cress seeds; paper towels; two saucers.

▲ Wet the paper towels. Line the saucers with them.

▲ Sprinkle cress seeds on both saucers.

▲ Put one saucer in a warm place. Put the other saucer in a refrigerator.

▲ Look at the seeds each day.

▲ Do not let the paper towels dry out.

▲ What happens? Do cress seeds grow best in a warm place or a cold place?

▲ Try growing some other seeds in the same way.

Hairy clowns

You will need: three clean yoghurt pots; cotton wool or paper towels; cress seeds or grass seeds; felt-tipped pens; a pencil.

▲ Draw a face on each pot.

▲ Fill the pots with cotton wool or paper towels.

▲ Wet the cotton wool or paper towels in two of the pots.

▲ Sprinkle seeds on all three pots.

▲ Put one of the pots with wet cotton wool or towels in a dark cupboard.

▲ Put the other two pots on a sunny window-sill.

▲ Do all three clowns grow hair?

▲ Do all three lots of seeds grow the same?

Food from plants

You will need: a pencil.

We can eat the parts of some plants.

▲ Tick the right box for the part we eat.

		Leaves	Roots	Fruit	Seeds
Carrots					
Apples					
Lettuce					
Plums					
Beetroot					
Cabbage					
Peas					
Grapes					
Peanuts					

Name _____

Fruit and vegetables

You will need: a pencil.

▲ Which is a fruit? Write f in the box.

▲ Find out where each of these grows. Do they grow in the ground, on a tree, or on a smaller plant?

SCHOLASTIC
www.scholastic.co.uk

Which seeds do birds like best?

You will need: small lids; a plank of wood; a hammer; small nails; seeds of different kinds; a pencil.

▲ Ask an adult to help you nail the lids on to a plank.

▲ Put different seeds in each lid.

▲ Put the plank on a lawn where the birds can see it.

▲ Watch carefully.

   Which seeds do the birds like best?

▲ Try the birds with some fruit.

   Which fruit do they like best?

▲ Record your results below.

The parts of a plant

You will need: a pencil; a ruler.

▲ Look at the picture.

▲ Join the names to the right parts of the plant.

root

shepherd's purse

stem

flower

fruit

seed

leaf

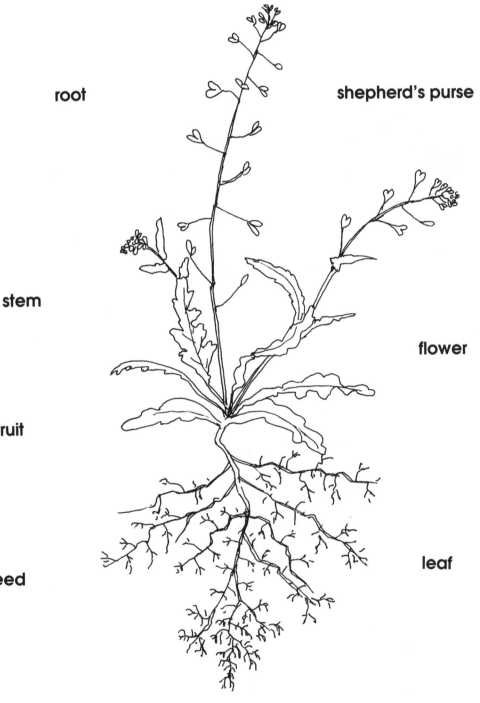

In the kitchen

This is Mr Jones' kitchen.
♣ Colour in the things in his kitchen using the key opposite.

metal – blue
wood – brown
glass – yellow

plastic – red
textiles – green
china or pottery – orange

In the classroom

This is Davinder's classroom.

❖ Use this colour code opposite to colour in the picture.

❖❖ Choose another material, colour it in green and add it to the key.

red – plastic   brown – wood
yellow – paper   blue – metal
green –

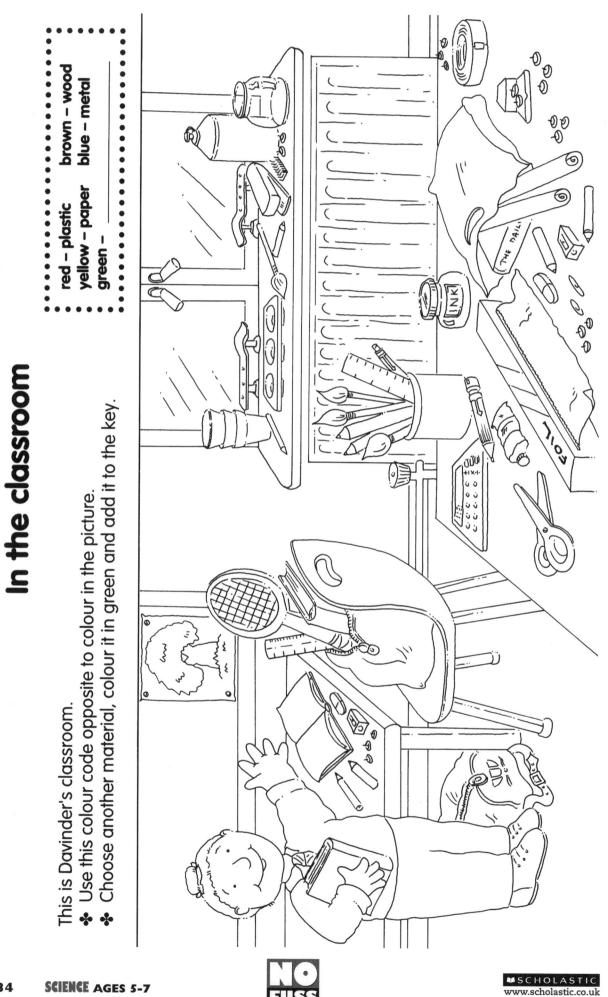

Name _____

Comparing materials

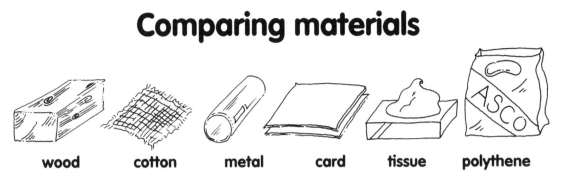

wood   cotton   metal   card   tissue   polythene

❖ Draw a picture of each material in the correct column.

Shiny	Dull

Feels cold	Feels warm

Bendy	Stiff

Waterproof	Soaks up water

Name _____

Packaging with paper

You will need: a pencil.

▲Look out for the goods we buy which are packaged in paper or card.

▲Draw a circle round all the goods in the picture below which are packaged in paper or card.

▲Add your own ideas on the back of this sheet.

▲Make a collection of paper and card packaging. Find ways of sorting them.

Name _____

Paper for mopping up spills

You will need: different kinds of paper used for mopping up spills, such as paper towels, tissues and kitchen roll; trays or plates; a magnifying glass; scissors; water.

▲ Cut all the paper to the same size.

▲ Use a magnifying glass to look closely at the paper.

▲ Which paper feels thick? Do any have more than one layer?

▲ Which do you think will mop up the most water?

▲ To find out, take a piece of paper and dip it in water. Shake the paper. Then squeeze out the water on to a tray. Do this with all types of paper. Which one soaked up the most water?

▲ Which is the best paper for mopping up spills?

Which fabric keeps you warm?

You will need: three pieces of fabric the same size, such as wool, cotton and nylon; four drinks cans; a funnel; water which is hot but **not** boiling.

▲Wrap one can in each type of fabric.

▲Ask an adult to pour the same amount of hot water into each can. Leave them for 15 minutes.

▲Take the covers off the cans. Which can feels the warmest?

▲Draw the coverings on the pictures below and write down what happened.

▲Which fabric would keep you warm in winter?

Name _____

Keeping warm and keeping cool

▲Look at the drawings of clothes below.

▲Put a red ring round the clothes which keep you warm and
a blue ring round the clothes which help you to keep cool.

T-shirt
coat
shorts
woolly hat
socks
gloves
bikini
sun hat
scarf

▲Make a list of the clothes you are wearing today.

▲Are they clothes that keep you warm or cool? What is
the weather like today?

Name _____

What do magnets attract?

You will need: a bar magnet.

▲ Move around the classroom with your magnet.
  • Touch objects with the magnet.
  • Which objects stick to the magnet?

▲ Draw or write your answers below.

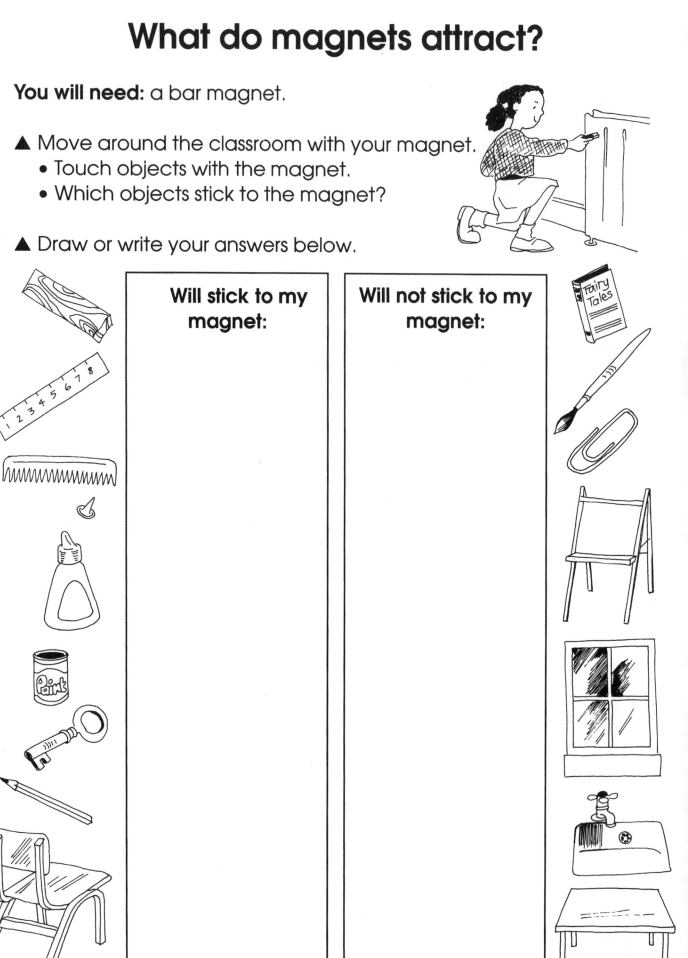

Will stick to my magnet:	Will not stick to my magnet:

SCHOLASTIC
www.scholastic.co.uk

Name _____

Is it magnetic?

You will need: a bar magnet; the objects named below.

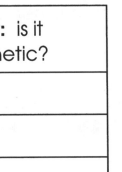

▲ Which things will be attracted to a magnet? Predict first, then use your magnet to find out if you were right.

▲ Record your results on the chart below.

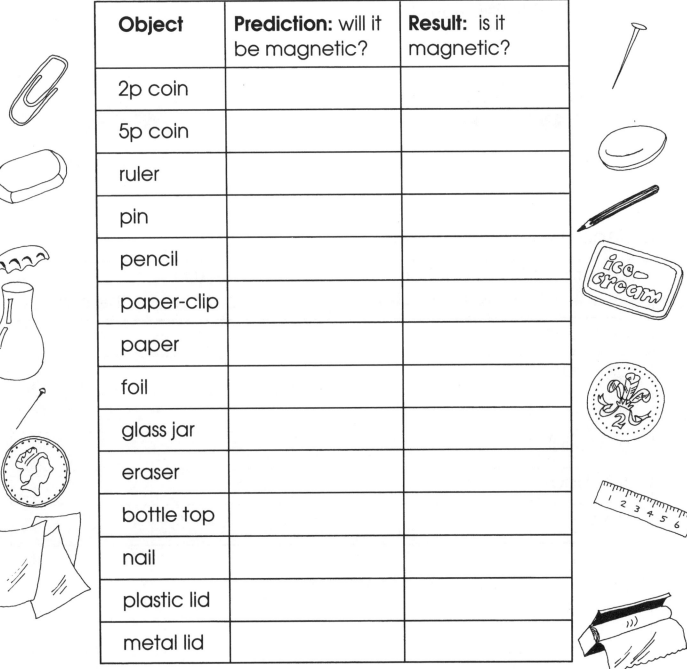

Object	Prediction: will it be magnetic?	Result: is it magnetic?
2p coin		
5p coin		
ruler		
pin		
pencil		
paper-clip		
paper		
foil		
glass jar		
eraser		
bottle top		
nail		
plastic lid		
metal lid		

▲ Discuss your results with a friend. What did you find out?

Will magnets work through some objects?

You will need: a magnet; paper-clip; the objects named below.

▲ Place the magnet on one side of the object and a paper-clip on the other side.
  • Now try to move the clip with the magnet.
  • Try some other objects.

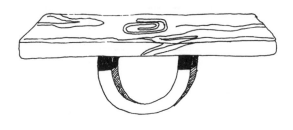

▲ Record your results below:

Object	Prediction: will it move the clip?	Result: did it move the clip?
plastic lid		
glass jar		
wood		
metal lid		
thin book		
card		
paper		
foil		

Make your own magnet

You will need: a magnet; nail or needle; paper-clips or pins.

▲ Stroke the nail in one direction with the magnet.
Lift the magnet clear of the nail before
starting another stroke.

▲ Now try to pick up a paper-clip with the nail.
  • How many clips will it pick up?
  • Is it as strong as the original magnet?
  • How long does it stay a magnet?
  • How could you make a nail a stronger magnet?

▲ Find out what other objects you can turn into a magnet!

Name _____

Day and night

You will need: a pencil; coloured pencils or crayons.

This picture is of daytime.

▲ Draw the same place at night.

▲ Say how it is different.

▲ Colour both pictures.

▲ How many things can you think of which give out light?

Name _____

What causes night and day?

You will need: a pencil; a globe or a large ball; a desk lamp or a torch. Work in a darkened room.

▲ Stand the globe or ball on the table.

▲ Shine the light on to it as shown in the picture below.

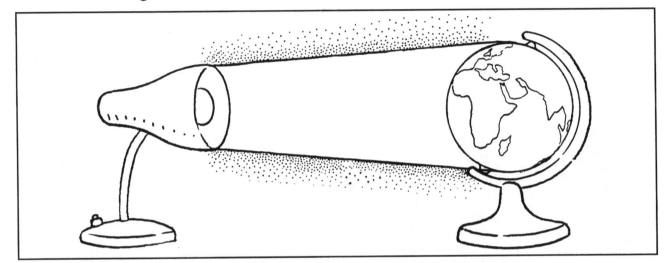

▲ Pretend the lamp or torch is the Sun.
  • Which part of the globe is light?
  • Which part is dark?

▲ Draw what you see.

▲ Slowly turn the globe or ball. Write down what you see.

▲ What causes day and night?

Shiny and not shiny

❖ Draw a line from each object to the correct word: **shiny** or **not shiny**.

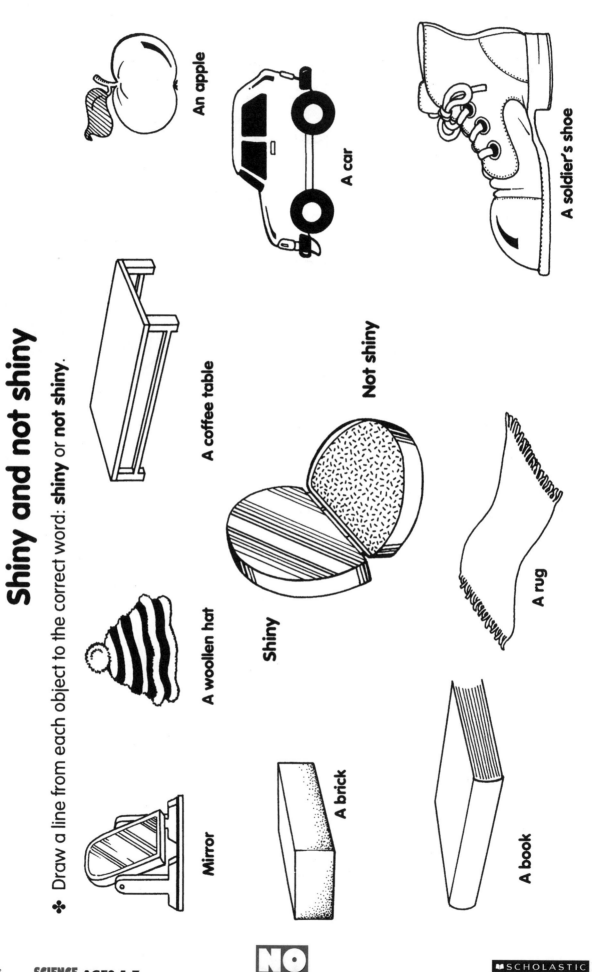

An apple

A car

A soldier's shoe

A coffee table

Not shiny

A woollen hat

Shiny

A rug

Mirror

A brick

A book

SCHOLASTIC
www.scholastic.co.uk

Name _____

Shiny things

You will need: a pencil.

▲ Make a collection of shiny things. Light bounces off these things. We say they **reflect** light.

▲ Look at your collection carefully. In which ones can you see your face?

▲ Look at the picture below carefully.
   • Put a tick against the objects you think are shiny.
   • Which of them do you think you could see your face in?

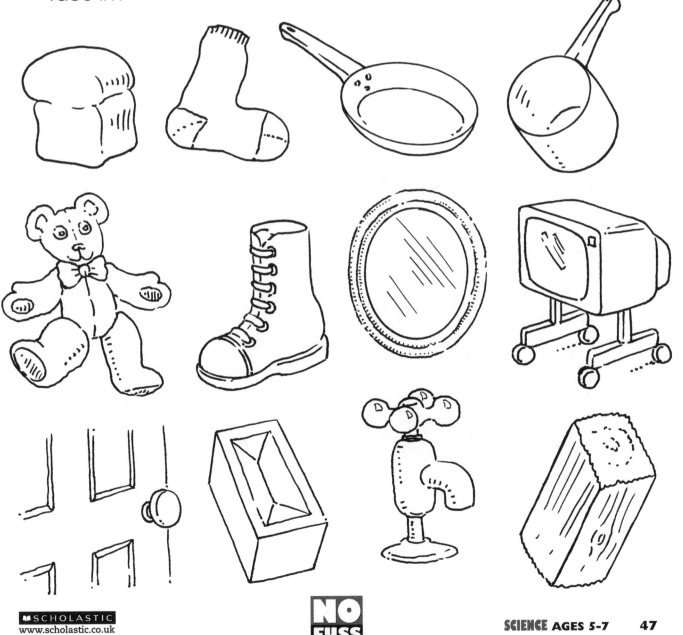

Shadow matching

You will need: a pencil; a ruler.

▲ Look carefully at the pictures below.

▲ Draw a line to join each picture to its shadow.

▲ Draw some shadow shapes of your own.

Letting light pass through

You will need: a coloured picture; some sheets of polythene; a pencil.

▲ Fix the picture on the wall.

▲ Hold a sheet of polythene in front of it. Can you still see the picture? If you can, the polythene is transparent.

▲ Now hold two sheets of polythene in front of the picture. Can you still see the picture?

▲ How many sheets of polythene must there be before you cannot see the picture?

▲ What have you learned about polythene?

▲ Find other materials which behave like this.

Making forces

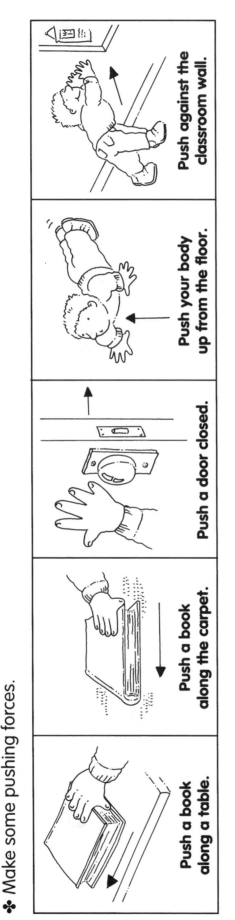

❖ Make some pushing forces.

Push against the classroom wall.

Push your body up from the floor.

Push a door closed.

Push a book along the carpet.

Push a book along a table.

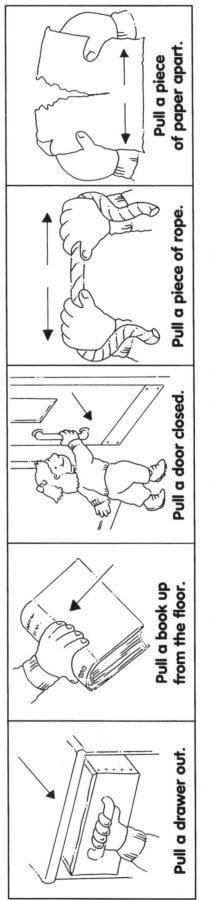

❖ Make some pulling forces.

Pull a piece of paper apart.

Pull a piece of rope.

Pull a door closed.

Pull a book up from the floor.

Pull a drawer out.

❖ Write down: the three largest forces you used; the three smallest forces you used; and the two forces you made which **did not move** anything.

Name _____

Push or pull?

You will need: scissors.

▲ We can make things work or move by pushing or pulling them.

▲ Sort these objects into two groups – those you push to make them work and those you pull.

▲ Find pictures of other things which you need to push or pull to make them work.

Pushes and pulls in the classroom

▲ Look around your classroom. Find things that you have to push or pull to make them work or move.

▲ Draw or write down the objects you find.

Objects we **push:**

Objects we **pull:**

NO FUSS
PHOTOCOPIABLE

Name _____

Lifting things

You will need: a string or thin rope; a cotton reel; a small plastic bucket; heavy objects such as toy bricks; wire; a hook placed at child height.

▲ Fill the bucket with heavy objects.

▲ Lift the bucket with one hand. How difficult is it to move?

▲ Now use both hands. Is this easier?

▲ Make a triangle from wire and attach a cotton reel.

▲ Hang the wire from a hook.

▲ Tie the string to the bucket.

▲ Wind the string over the cotton reel. You have made a pulley.

▲ Pull on the string to lift the bucket.
  • Is it easier to lift the bucket now?
  • Can you make it easier using more cotton reels?

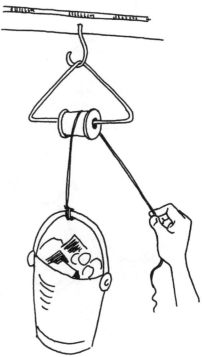

Make it move!

The objects below all have something missing that would
stop them from moving.
▲ Draw the missing parts.

▲ Draw some other objects with the moving part missing.
Ask a friend to draw the missing part.

SCHOLASTIC
www.scholastic.co.uk

Name _____

Using ramps

You will need: a toy car; a length of wood or a large book; a ruler; measuring tape; books; large floor space.

▲ Place the wood on some books 10cm high so that it makes a slope. Place a toy car on the ramp and let it go.

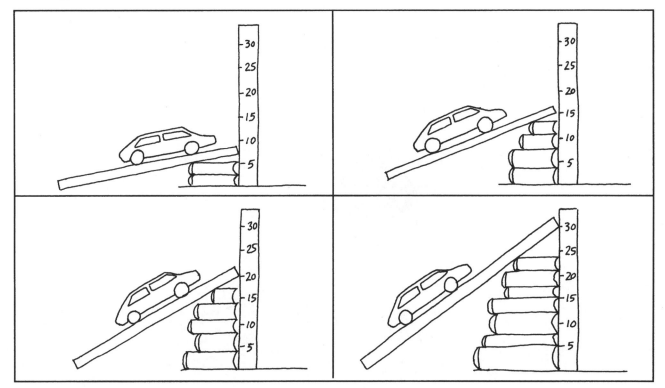

▲ Measure the distance from the end of the ramp to where the car stopped and record your results on the chart below.

Height of ramp (cm)	Distance car travelled (cm)
10 cm	
15 cm	
20 cm	
30 cm	

▲ Do the same thing with ramps 15cm, 20cm and 30cm high. What do you notice?

▲ On which ramp does the car roll furthest? Can you work out why?

▲ Try other objects on the slope. Which ones travel furthest?

Friction

You will need: a large book; a metal tray; a piece of wood; a piece of wood covered with fabric or sandpaper; an eraser.

▲ Lean the book against some other books so that it forms a slope.

▲ Place the eraser on the slope and watch how it moves. Does it slide freely?

▲ Keep the books in place. Try the eraser on the metal tray, the wood, the fabric or sandpaper.
- On which surface does the eraser slide best?
- Can you work out why?

▲ Discuss your results with a friend.

▲ Try out other objects on different surfaces.

www.scholastic.co.uk

Name _____

Will it bounce?

You will need: a metre ruler or measuring tape fixed to the wall; the objects listed below. Work with a friend.

▲ Look at the list of objects below.

▲ Predict which objects will bounce.

▲ Drop each object from the same height on to a wooden or tiled floor. Use a metre ruler to measure how high they bounced.
 • Why do some bounce better than others?
 • Why do some things not bounce at all?

Object	Prediction: will it bounce?	Result: how high did it bounce?
marble		
tennis ball		
ball of Plasticine		
netball		
ball of paper		
golf ball		
cricket ball		
dice		
ping-pong ball		

▲ Try out some more objects.

Sink or float?

You will need: a bowl or bucket of water; the objects listed below.

▲ Look at the objects listed below.

▲ Predict whether you think each object will float or sink.

▲ Test each one to see if you were right.

Object	Prediction: will it sink or float?	Result: did it sink or float?
paper-clip		
marble		
bean seed		
plastic ruler		
wood		
spoon		
glass jar		
wooden peg		
foil tray		

▲ Now try out other objects.

Does shape affect floating?

You will need: a bowl or bucket of water; Plasticine.

▲ Make the Plasticine into the shapes shown below.
▲ Put each shape in the water. What happens?

Shape		Result : sink or float?
○	ball shape	
⬯	sausage shape	
▱	flat shape	
⬚	cube shape	

▲ Now make a boat from the Plasticine.
▲ Draw the boat you made in the space below.
Did it float?

▲ Experiment with different boat shapes. Draw them and say whether they sank or floated.

▲ How does shape affect whether it sinks or floats?

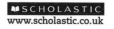

Name _____

Everyday sounds

▲ Listen carefully. What sounds can you hear?
▲ Are they loud or soft sounds?
▲ Fill in the table of sounds.

Loud sounds	Soft sounds
motorbike	whisper

▲ Which sound do you like best? _____
▲ Why?_____

Loud and soft sounds

▲ Do the things below make loud sounds or soft sounds?
▲ Write or draw them in the right box.

Loud sounds	Soft sounds

▲ Think of some other objects that make loud or soft sounds.
▲ Write their names in the boxes.

Which animal?

✤ Link the sound to the animal.

Sound words

Here are some sound words.

▲ Put the right word by the picture.

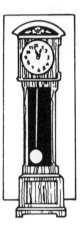

▲ Write down some more sound words. Draw a picture below for one of them.

Sounds from different surfaces

You will need: a coin; a ruler.

▲ Drop a coin on the table.

▲ Drop a coin on the floor.

▲ Drop a coin on the carpet.

▲ When does the coin make a loud sound?
▲ When does the coin make a soft sound?
▲ Cut out the pictures above and put them in order with the loudest first.

Name _____

One ear or two?

You will need: a friend to work with; a triangle.

▲ Listen with one ear. Close your eyes. Point to the sound.

▲ Listen with two ears. Close your eyes. Point to the sound.
Are two ears better than one?

▲ Draw an animal using his ears to listen with.

Make a stethoscope

You will need: a plastic tube; two funnels.

The doctor listens to soft sounds.
She listens with a stethoscope.

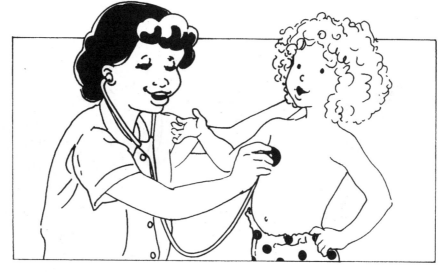

▲ Make your own stethoscope.

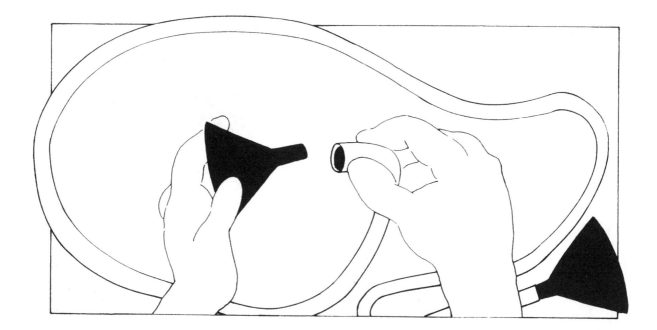

▲ What soft sounds can you hear with it?
▲ Make a list of the sounds you can hear.
▲ Can you hear soft sounds with a cardboard tube?

■SCHOLASTIC
www.scholastic.co.uk

Name _____

Make your own telephone

You will need: a friend to work with; two plastic pots; a long piece of thin string; two matchsticks.

▲ Ask an adult to make a hole in the bottom of each pot.

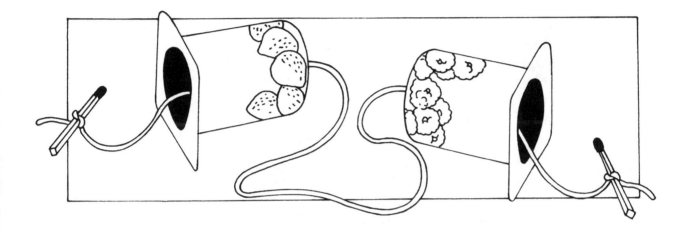

▲ Ask a friend to put one pot to his or her ear.
▲ Pull the string tight.
▲ Speak into your pot.

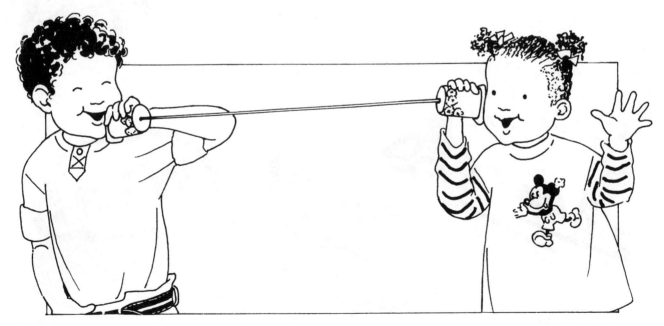

▲ Can your friend hear you?
▲ Can you make a telephone with three pots?

Match the sounds

▲ Match these sounds. Draw a line to the right picture.

Name _____

You as a baby

You will need: a pencil.

▲ Find out all you can about yourself when you were a baby.

When were you born? _____

Where were you born? _____

How much did you weigh?_____

What was your hair like?_____

When did you first walk?_____

What was your first word? _____

What toys did you play with?_____

Have you a picture of yourself when you were a baby?

Growing

You will need: a pencil.

As we grow, we get bigger. It takes time to grow.

▲ Look at these children.

Caroline is 6 months old.
Petra is 6 years old.
Kevin is 14 years old.
Sanjit is 1 year old.
Kirsty is 2 years old.

▲ Write each of the children's names under their picture.

▲ Draw some of the clothes Caroline might wear.
▲ Draw some of the clothes Petra might wear.

SCHOLASTIC
www.scholastic.co.uk

Name _____

Me and my friends

You will need: a pencil; a tape measure; bathroom scales.

Work with some friends.

▲ Fill in this chart.

name	boy or girl	age	hair colour	height	weight

▲ Can you find anyone exactly like you?

Food

You will need: a pencil; a ruler.

Some foods give us energy.

Some foods help to us grow.

Some foods keep us healthy.

▲ Which of these foods have you eaten today?

_____

_____

▲ Which foods do you like the best?

_____

_____

▲ Colour the foods that keep us healthy.

SCHOLASTIC
www.scholastic.co.uk

Types of food

You should eat only small amounts of food coloured red.
You should eat medium amounts of foods coloured green.
You should eat lots of food not coloured.

❖ Colour in red all foods with an S on them.
❖ Colour in green all foods with an M on them.

❖ Tell a teacher or a friend the foods you
should eat a little of, a little more of and a lot of.

Using medicines

✤ Which medicine might an adult give you for:

a cough?

a cut?

an upset stomach?

a headache?

tooth coming through?

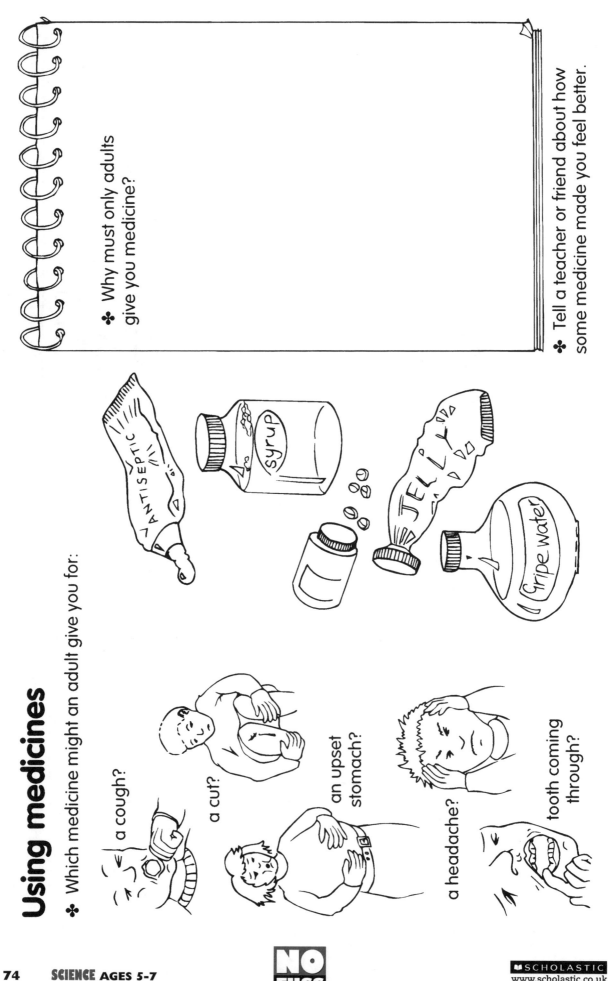

❖ Why must only adults give you medicine?

❖ Tell a teacher or friend about how some medicine made you feel better.

■SCHOLASTIC
www.scholastic.co.uk

Name _____

How good is your memory?

You will need: a pencil; a clock with a second hand.

How much can you remember?

▲ Look carefully at this picture for one minute. Now cover the picture. How many of the things can you remember in two minutes? Write them down.

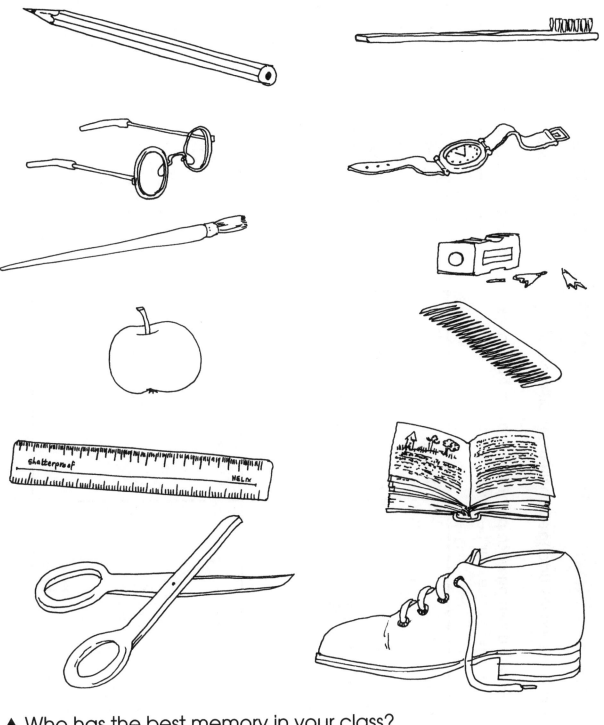

▲ Who has the best memory in your class?

Stems and leaves

How are leaves arranged on stems in different plants?

How are leaves and flower stems arranged?

✤ Look at a buttercup then tick the correct box.

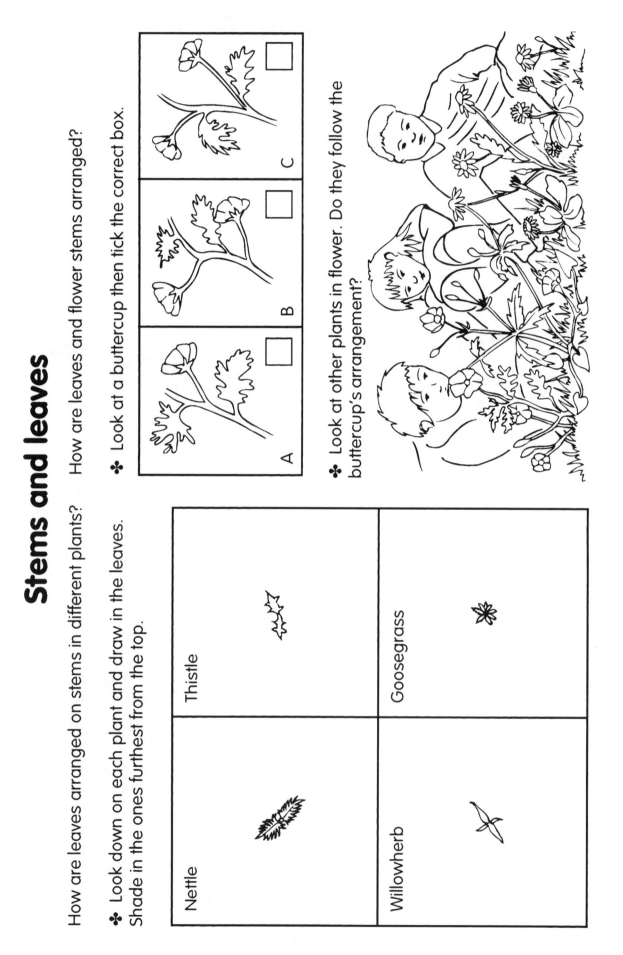

A ☐   B ☐   C ☐

✤ Look at other plants in flower. Do they follow the buttercup's arrangement?

✤ Look down on each plant and draw in the leaves. Shade in the ones furthest from the top.

Nettle	Thistle
Willowherb	Goosegrass

Name _____

✤ What do the parts labelled A to L do?

✤ Look through the table and match each part with a task. Part L has two tasks.

The part	What it does
	Makes food
	Takes water to leaf
	Attracts insects
	Holds up flowers
	Takes water to leaf and flower
	Catches pollen
	Turns into a seed
	Attracts animals to eat it
	Grows into new plant
	Holds plant in ground
	Protects flower in bud
	Takes up water from soil

What the plant's parts do

✤ Look at the parts labelled by the letters. Which letter is labelling

a petal _____

stamen _____

stigma _____

ovule _____

seed _____

How seeds get away

✤ Look at a collection of fruits and sort them into these groups.

You will need:
a collection of fruits

Carried away by water

Pod twists and shoots out seed

Fruits stick to fur

Fruit flesh eaten but stone and pips thrown away by animal

Carried away by wind

Eaten and passed through an animal's body

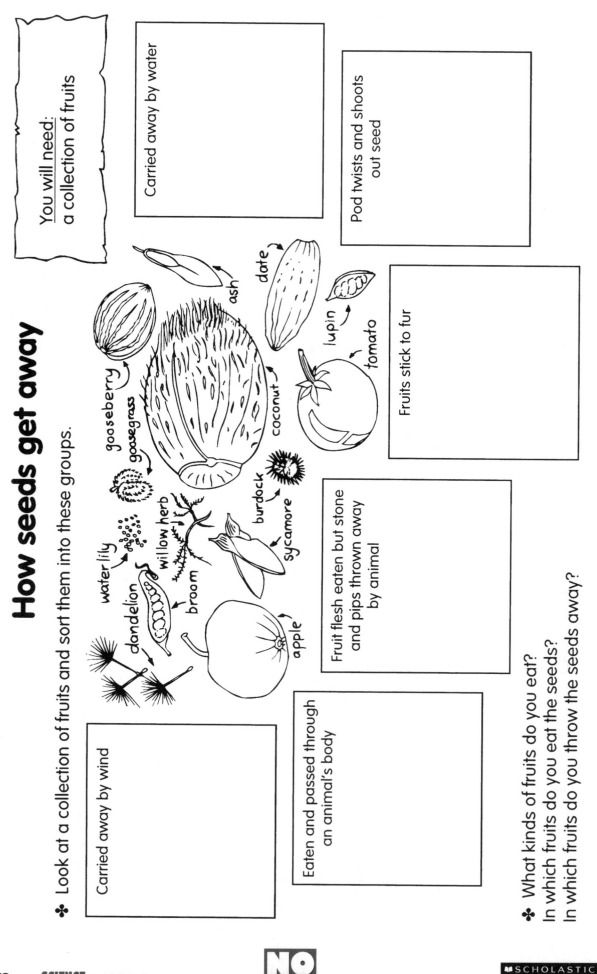

ash

date

lupin

tomato

coconut

gooseberry

goosegrass

water lily

willow herb

dandelion

broom

burdock

sycamore

apple

✤ What kinds of fruits do you eat?
In which fruits do you eat the seeds?
In which fruits do you throw the seeds away?

Name _____

Animals in the house 1

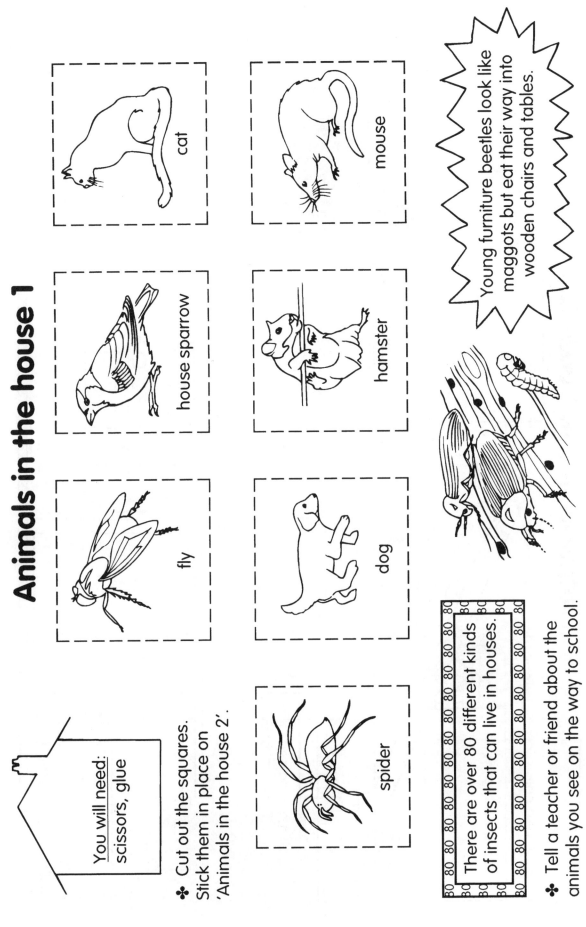

cat

mouse

house sparrow

hamster

fly

dog

spider

Young furniture beetles look like maggots but eat their way into wooden chairs and tables.

You will need: scissors, glue

♣ Cut out the squares. Stick them in place on 'Animals in the house 2'.

There are over 80 different kinds of insects that can live in houses.

♣ Tell a teacher or friend about the animals you see on the way to school.

Animals in the house 2

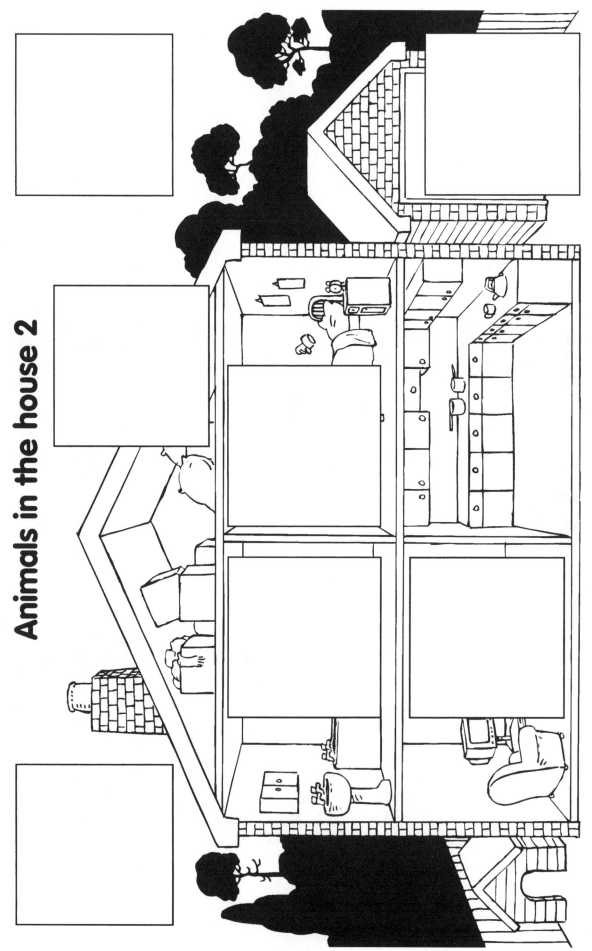

SCHOLASTIC
www.scholastic.co.uk

Wildlife in a park and a pond

✿ Find the home of each living thing and join them with a line.

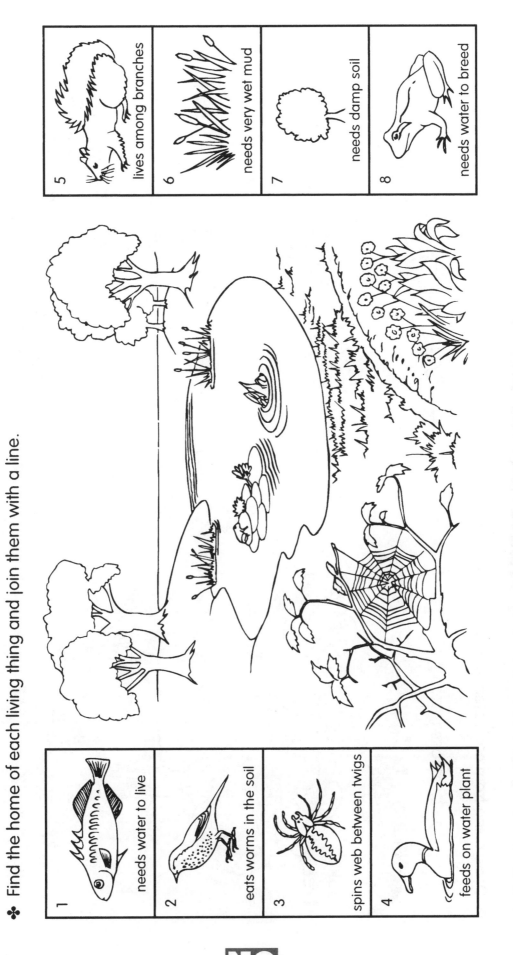

5 lives among branches	6 needs very wet mud
7 needs damp soil	8 needs water to breed

1 needs water to live	2 eats worms in the soil
3 spins web between twigs	4 feeds on water plant

✿ Tell a teacher or friend how living in a pond is different from living in a park.

Where plants live

✿ Draw a line from each plant to the place where it lives.

flower bed

waste ground

park

pavement flags

rotten log

lawn

thistle

tulip

daisy

toadstool

moss

oak tree

✿ Tell a teacher or friend about all the plants you see on the way to school.

SCHOLASTIC
www.scholastic.co.uk

Name _____

The main groups of living things

You will need:
scissors, glue, plain paper
coloured pens or crayons

✤ Cut out these pictures and arrange them into groups.

conifer	starfish	sponges	reptiles
green	no backbone	no backbone	backbone

algae (seaweed)	fish	arthropods	amphibians
green	backbone	no backbone	backbone

mosses and liverworts	segmented worms	flowering plant	molluscs
green	no backbone	green	no backbone

mammals	jellyfish	birds	ferns and horse tails
backbone	no backbone	backbone	green

There are over two million different kinds of living thing on the earth.

NO FUSS
PHOTOCOPIABLE

Name _____

Planning a wildlife area

Small Town Primary School is planning a wildlife area in the school grounds. Help them decide where everything should go.

✿ Cut out each item below and put it on the map in the best place.

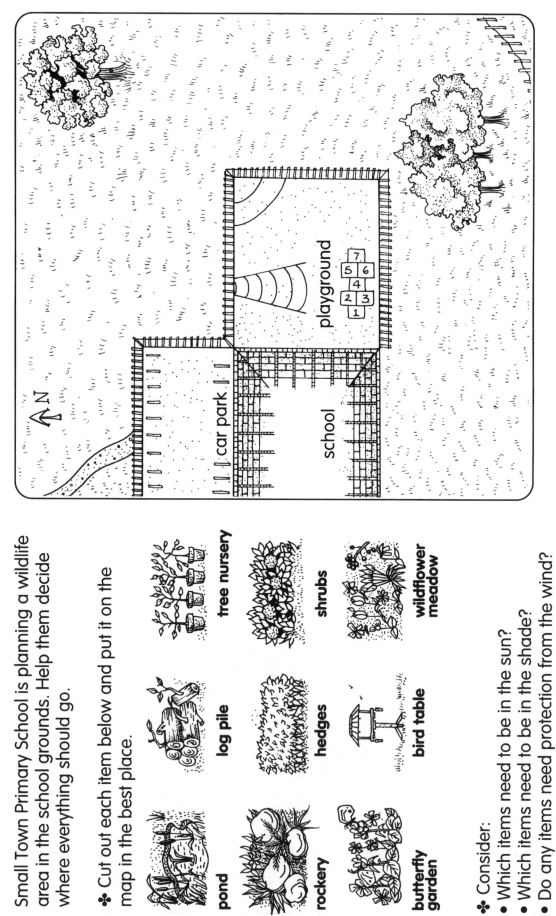

pond

rockery

butterfly garden

log pile

hedges

bird table

tree nursery

shrubs

wildflower meadow

✿ Consider:
• Which items need to be in the sun?
• Which items need to be in the shade?
• Do any items need protection from the wind?

NO FUSS PHOTOCOPIABLE

Name _____

Living and non-living

You will need: a pencil; coloured pencils or crayons.

▲ Look at the pictures. Which of them are of living things?
▲ Colour the living things.

▲ Using the back of this page, make a list of some more living things.

Name _____

Signs of life

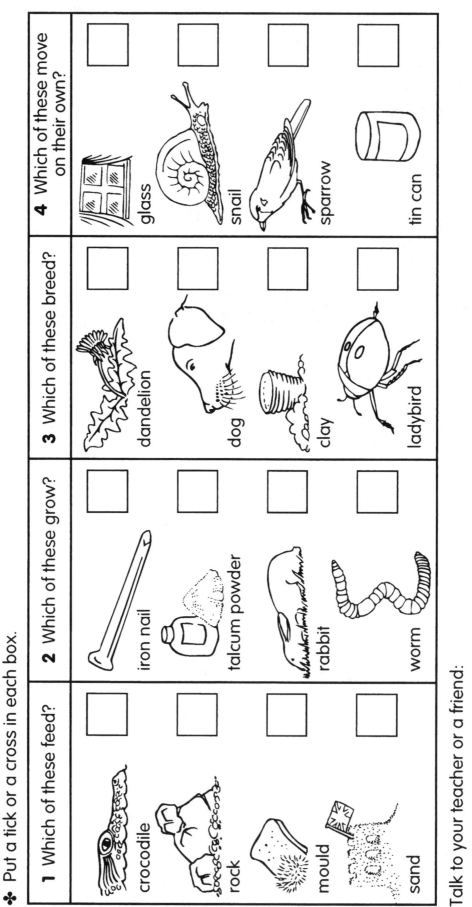

✤ Put a tick or a cross in each box.

1 Which of these feed?

☐ crocodile

☐ rock

☐ mould

☐ sand

2 Which of these grow?

☐ iron nail

☐ talcum powder

☐ rabbit

☐ worm

3 Which of these breed?

☐ dandelion

☐ dog

☐ clay

☐ ladybird

4 Which of these move on their own?

☐ glass

☐ snail

☐ sparrow

☐ tin can

Talk to your teacher or a friend:

✤ What else do living things do?

✤ How can you tell that a mouse is a living thing?

Name _____

What do you know about humans?

✤ Name the parts of the body shown in a, b and c.

✤ Choose from this list: neck, shoulder, arm, knee, back, elbow, leg.

a

b

c

A   B   C   D

✤ Put a circle around the things you need to stay alive

light   food   home   stones   water

✤ Name a medicine that makes you better. What illness does it help?

✤ Write down the letters in order to show the human life cycle.

✤ Name the sense shown in each picture.

① ② ③ ④ ⑤ ⑥

Measuring hands

You will need: some squared paper; beads or marbles; a pencil.

▲ Put your hand on the paper. Draw round your hand. Count the squares in your hand picture. (Do not count very small parts of a square.)

Write down: My hand covers_____ squares.

▲ Here is another way of measuring your hand. See how many marbles you can pick up with it.

▲ Who has the biggest hands in your class?_____

▲ Whose hands are the smallest?_____

Animals and their young

♣ Draw a line from each young animal to the animal it will grow into.

♣ Which animals change the most as they grow?

♣ Tell a teacher or friend about how your pet changed as it grew up.

The frog life cycle

Another frog has a tadpole 26cm long.

One kind of frog keeps its tadpoles in its throat.

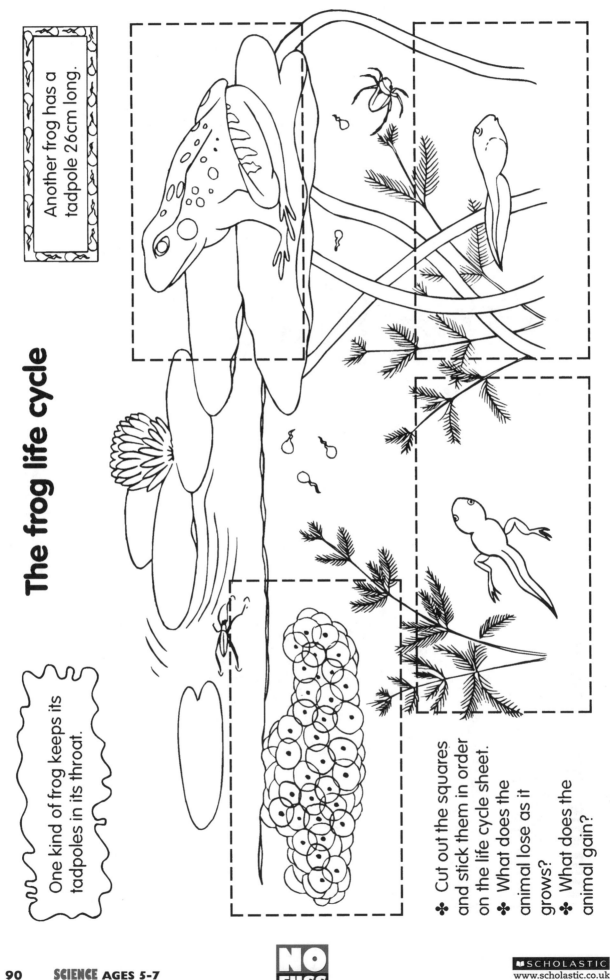

✤ Cut out the squares and stick them in order on the life cycle sheet.
✤ What does the animal lose as it grows?
✤ What does the animal gain?

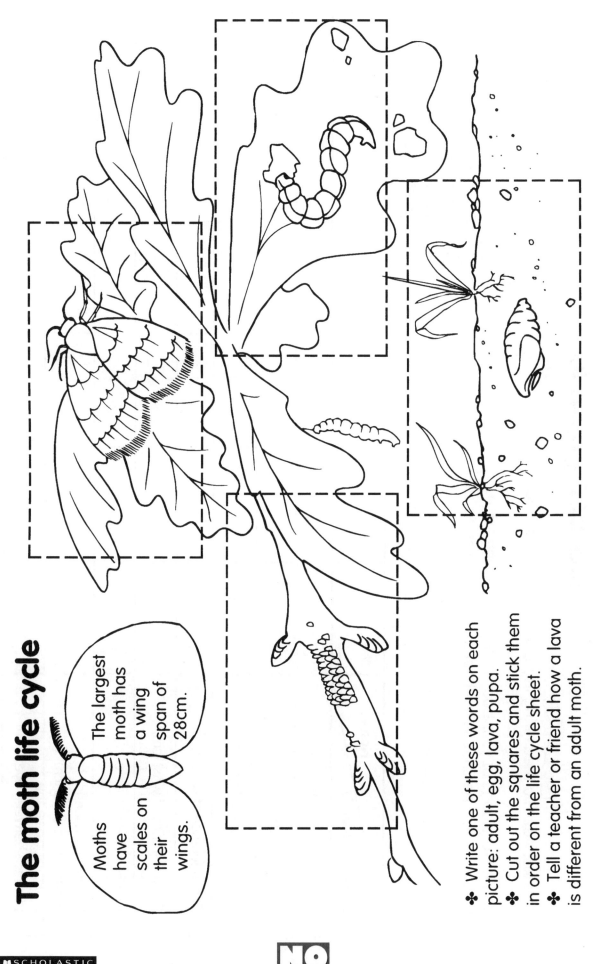

The moth life cycle

The largest moth has a wing span of 28cm.

Moths have scales on their wings.

✤ Write one of these words on each picture: adult, egg, lava, pupa.
✤ Cut out the squares and stick them in order on the life cycle sheet.
✤ Tell a teacher or friend how a lava is different from an adult moth.

Measuring people

You will need: a measuring tape, a metre ruler, a small ruler.

✤ Measure parts of your body and complete the table below. Each time choose the best measuring instrument.

♣ Do the same for some friends.

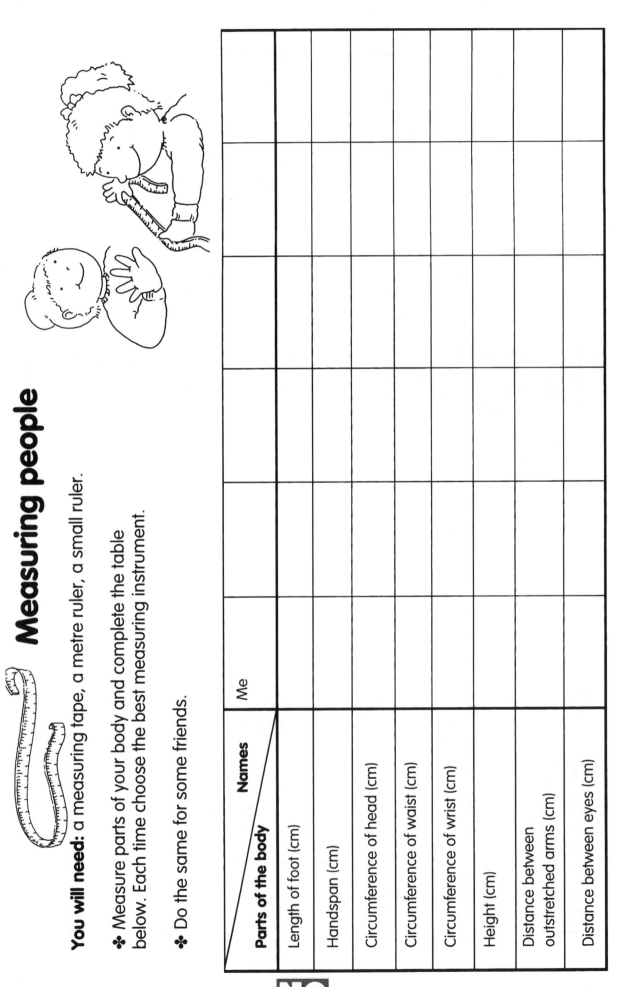

Parts of the body \ Names	Me						
Length of foot (cm)							
Handspan (cm)							
Circumference of head (cm)							
Circumference of waist (cm)							
Circumference of wrist (cm)							
Height (cm)							
Distance between outstretched arms (cm)							
Distance between eyes (cm)							

SCHOLASTIC
www.scholastic.co.uk

How big are your lungs?

When you take a deep breath you fill your lungs with air.

✱ How much air does it take to fill your lungs? Do this experiment to find out.

You will need: some plastic tubing, a small polythene bag.

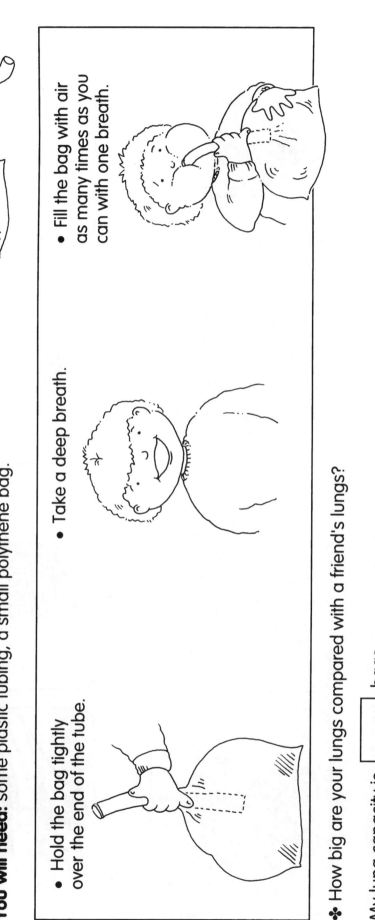

- Take a deep breath.

- Fill the bag with air as many times as you can with one breath.

- Hold the bag tightly over the end of the tube.

Take care!

✿ How big are your lungs compared with a friend's lungs?

My lung capacity is [ ] bags.

My friend's lung capacity is [ ] bags.

Name _____

What are these things made from?

✤ Match each raw material on the top row with the correct end product on the bottom row.

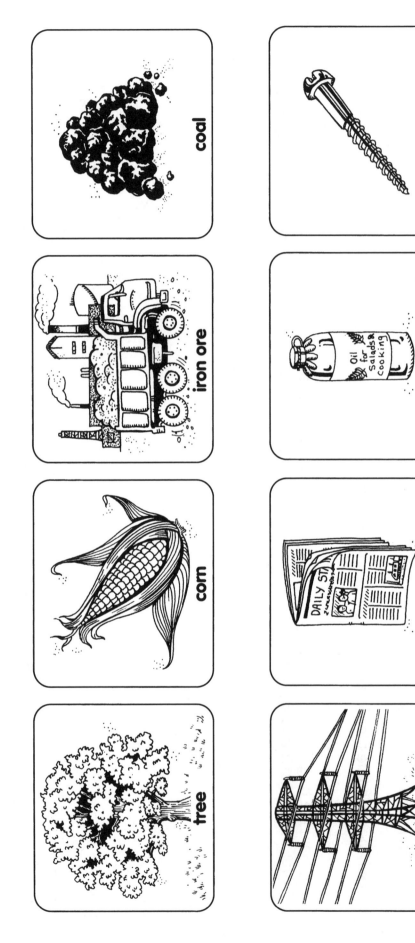

coal

iron ore

corn

tree

steel screw

cooking oil

newspaper

electricity

✤ Find out what a window, some curtains and a brick are made from.

SCHOLASTIC
www.scholastic.co.uk

Name _____

Making with materials

✤ Join each of the things below to the material from which it is made. One has already been done for you.

rubber	clay	iron and steel	cotton	plastic	glass	wood

tyre

scissors

pot

paper

bat

dress

drinking glass

elastic band

boat

✤ Now draw some more things and join them to the materials from which they are made.

Keeping cold

You will need: four small plastic bags; ice cubes; a collection of materials to wrap the bags in, for example, a woollen blanket, newspaper, foil, pieces of polythene; a timer.

Work with a friend.

Who can make an ice cube last the longest?

▲ Put one ice cube in each plastic bag.

▲ Put a different material round three of the bags. Do not put anything around the fourth bag.

▲ Put all the bags in the same place. Leave them for 15 minutes.

▲ Which bag kept the ice cubes the coolest?

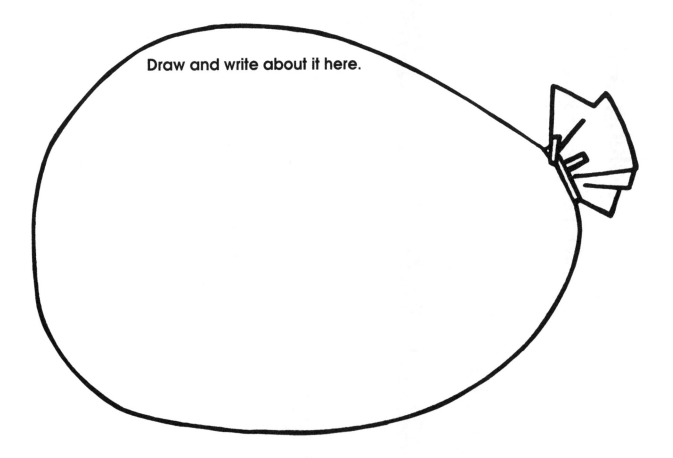

Draw and write about it here.

▲ How do you keep food cool when you go on a picnic?

SCHOLASTIC
www.scholastic.co.uk

An ice cube melting

You will need: ice cubes; warm water; salt; a mixture of salt and sand; small bowls; a timer.

▲ Put an ice cube on a saucer in a warm place. Look at it every few minutes. How long did it take to melt?

▲ How do you think you could melt an ice cube quickly? Try out your own ideas.

▲ Put an ice cube in each of the four bowls.

▲ Add warm water to one, salt to another, a mixture of sand and salt to another and nothing to the fourth.

▲ Put on the timer. How long does each ice cube take to melt? Which melts the quickest?

Draw and write about it here.

Name

The wrong substance

Each of these objects has been made with the wrong substance.
♣ Discuss with a friend, why each of these substances should not have been used.

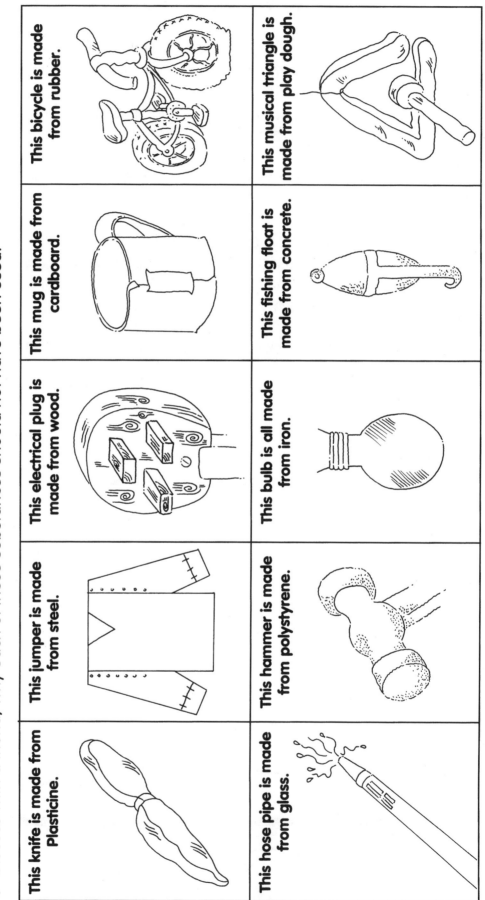

This bicycle is made from rubber.

This musical triangle is made from play dough.

This mug is made from cardboard.

This fishing float is made from concrete.

This electrical plug is made from wood.

This bulb is all made from iron.

This jumper is made from steel.

This hammer is made from polystyrene.

This knife is made from Plasticine.

This hose pipe is made from glass.

Name _____

What are you wearing today?

You will need: a hand lens; a pencil.

▲In the frame below, draw a picture of yourself wearing the clothes you have on today.

▲Find out what your clothes are made from.

▲Label your drawing with the names of the clothes and what they are made from.

▲Find out which are made from natural fibres, manufactured fibres or a mixture of both. You may need help with this.

Types of fabrics

You will need: a hand lens; examples of knitted, woven and tangled fabrics; scissors; glue.

Fabrics are made from fibres which are interlaced together. They can be:

Knitted	Woven	Tangled

▲Use a hand lens and the pictures shown above to help you find one fabric of each kind.

▲What can you find out about the different kinds of fabric?
- Try stretching them.
- Hold them up to the light. What can you see?
- Unravel some of the fabric to see how the fibres are interlaced.

▲Share what you have discovered with your friends.

▲Stick examples below and label them.

_____   _____   _____

SCHOLASTIC
www.scholastic.co.uk

Name _____

How strong are threads?

You will need: 30cm lengths of thread made from cotton, wool and nylon or other kinds of manufactured threads; a hook fixed in a low position to a wall; a small bucket; marbles or weights; sticky tape; a pencil.

▲ Sort out the threads into sets of wool threads, cotton threads and manufactured threads.

▲ Compare the look and feel of the threads.

▲ Test the strength of the threads by tying one end to the hook and the other to the handle of the bucket. Gradually put weights in the bucket until the thread breaks.

▲ Stick a sample of thread on to paper and write down how much the thread held.

▲ Test the other threads. Did they all break in the same way?
  • Were you unable to break some?
  • Which set had the strongest threads?
  • Are the threads as strong when wet?

Changing shapes

▲ We can change the shapes of some objects.

▲ Look at the objects below.

▲ Draw or write down how you could change the shape
of each object.

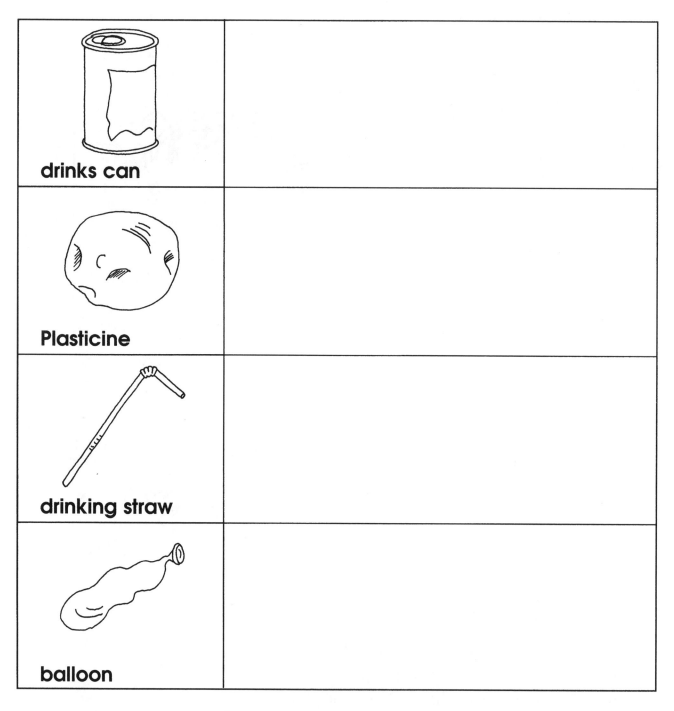

drinks can	
Plasticine	
drinking straw	
balloon	

▲ Make a collection of other objects that can change shape.

Name _____

Marbles and moving air

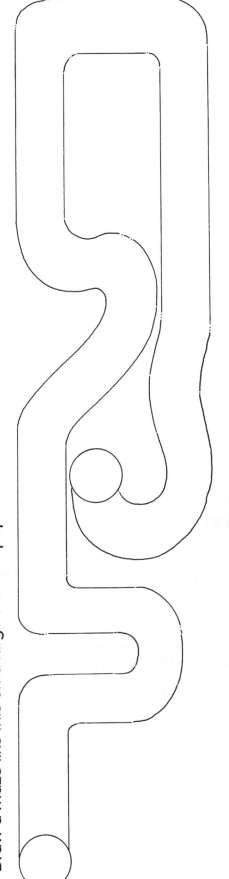

You will need: a drinking straw, a marble.

If you blow down the straw, the moving air will make a **force**. Forces can make things **move**, **stop** and **change direction**.

❖ Use this force to make the marble move.

❖ Now roll the marble along this line. Use the force of the air to make the marble stop on the spot. Do not touch the marble.

❖ Draw a maze like this on a large sheet of paper.

❖ Use your force of moving air to make the marble follow the maze.

Feeling the 'push' of water

You will need: a ping-pong ball; a jar or tank of water; various weights 1g–50g; sticky tape; masking/coloured tape.

▲ Put some water in the tank. Mark the water level with masking tape on the outside of the container.

▲ Put the ball in the water. What happens?

▲ Now push down on the ball with your hand. Try to make the ball sink.
  • What can you feel?
  • What happens to the water level when your hand goes into the water?
  • Why does this happen?

▲ Now attach weights to the ball and try to make it sink.
  • Predict the result before you try each weight.
  • Say what happens.

Weight	Prediction: will it sink?	Result: did it sink?	Water level: what happened?
1g			
5g			
10g			
20g			
50g			

NO FUSS
PHOTOCOPIABLE

Name _____

Is salty water best for floating?

You will need: Plasticine; plastic counters or cubes; a container of water (with clear sides); salt.

▲ Make a boat shape from the Plasticine.
  • Make sure it will float in the container of water.
  • Is it floating high or low in the water?

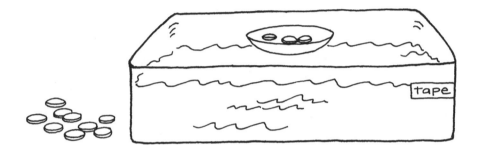

▲ Now add counters one at a time into the boat.
• Count how many counters it takes to sink the boat.

• Write your answer below:

It took ☐ counters to sink my boat.

▲ Now take the boat out of the water and dissolve lots of salt in the water.

▲ Put your boat in the water and do the experiment again. By now the boat will have absorbed some water and become heavier. Write your result below:

It took ☐ counters to sink my boat in salty water.

▲ Can you explain the result?

▲ Try other liquids such as cooking oil, milk or soft drinks. How well does the boat float?

NO FUSS
PHOTOCOPIABLE

Water safety

▲ Imagine that your friend has fallen into a swimming pool and cannot swim.

There are some objects nearby which you could throw in to help your friend to float in the water until help arrives.

▲ Put a tick next to any object below that would float if you threw it in to the water.

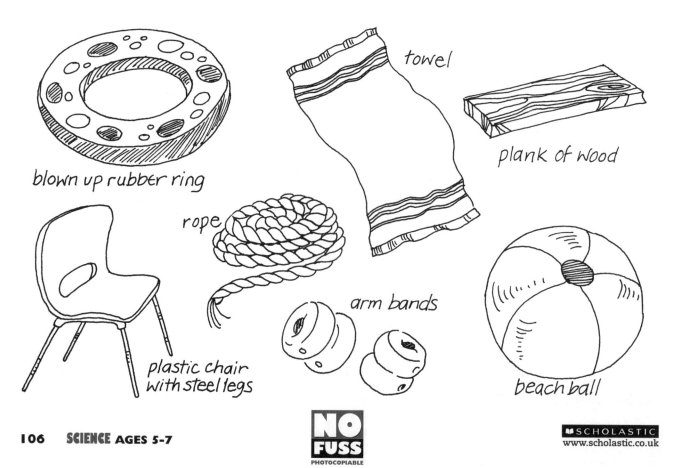

blown up rubber ring

towel

plank of wood

rope

plastic chair with steel legs

arm bands

beach ball

SCHOLASTIC
www.scholastic.co.uk

Stretch and twist

You will need: the objects shown below.

elastic band

drinking straw

copper wire

foil

wool

paper

balloon

tights

pipe cleaner

sticky tape

You can change the shape of some objects by stretching or twisting them.

▲ Try to stretch and twist each of the objects listed above.

▲ Draw or write down the objects that can stretch or twist in the spaces below.

Things that **stretch:**	Things that **twist:**

▲ Investigate whether other objects can be stretched or twisted.

NO FUSS
PHOTOCOPIABLE

Moving things

▲ **You will need:** a heavy book; string; round pencils; a piece of cloth.

▲ Place the cloth on the floor.
  • Try to push the book over it.
  • How easy is it to move?

▲ Place some pencils underneath the book.
  • Push the book along. (You will need to keep moving the back pencil to the front.)
  • Is the book easier to move now?

▲ Tie a long piece of string around the book.
  • Pull the book along the floor.
  • Is it easy to move?

▲ Try to push or pull other objects.
▲ Make a list of things we push to move and those we pull to move.

NO FUSS
PHOTOCOPIABLE

Rolling things

▲ **You will need:** the objects shown below; a smooth floor surface.

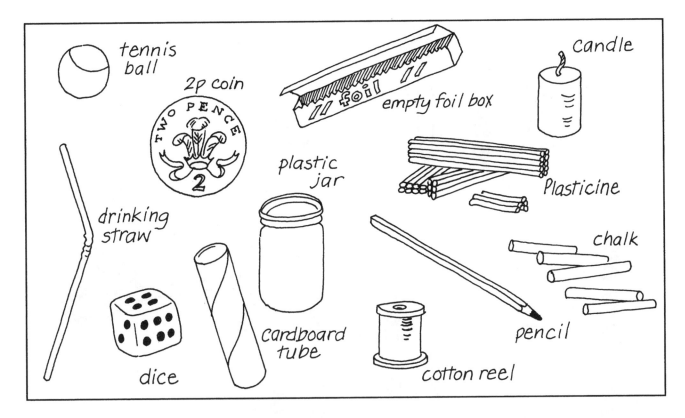

▲ Roll each object along the floor.
- Which object rolls best?
- What affects how the object rolls?
Size? Shape? Weight?

▲ Try rolling some other objects. Can they all roll?

How do your toys move?

✤ Join the toy to the word that helps you to describe how it moves.

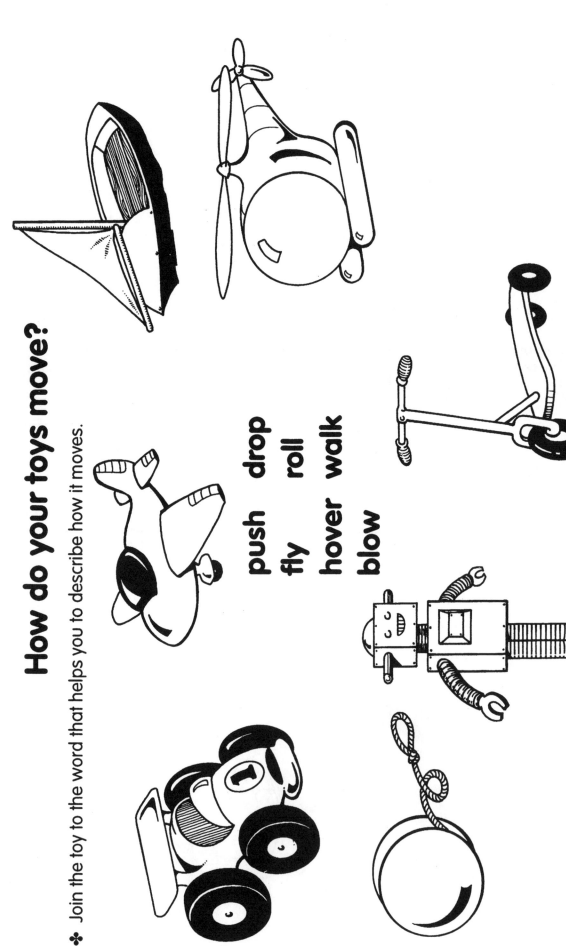

push   drop

fly   roll

hover   walk

blow

Easy mover

✤ Draw a line from each object to the correct part of the circle.

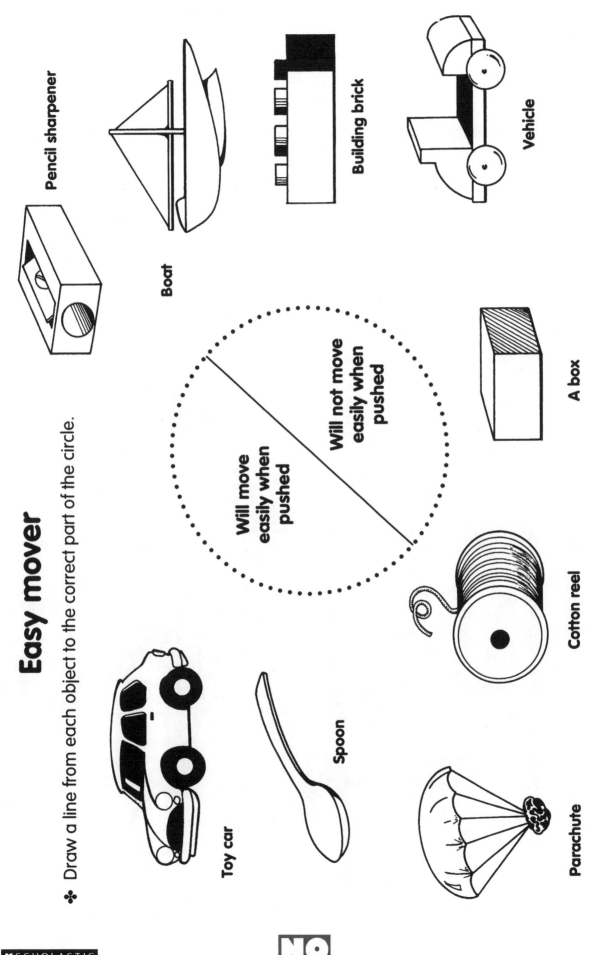

Pencil sharpener

Boat

Building brick

Vehicle

A box

Will move easily when pushed

Will not move easily when pushed

Cotton reel

Toy car

Spoon

Parachute

Make a buggy

You will need: a plastic ice-cream container; garden cane or dowelling rods; four cotton reels; drawing pins.

▲ Ask an adult to make a hole on each side of the ice-cream container large enough to push the cane rods through.

▲ Fix a cotton reel to the end of each cane and push in a drawing pin to stop the reel from coming off.

▲ Try making other types of wheels. Which ones work best?

The great escape

If a lorry's brakes fail the driver needs to find an escape route to slow the lorry down. Sometimes on steep hills there are special sand-pits called 'escape lanes' that the lorry can be driven into. The sand helps the lorry to stop.

YOU WILL NEED

- a toy lorry;
- a piece of wood or stiff card;
- books or building bricks (to raise the ramp);
- materials such as sand paper, corrugated card, fabrics – silk, velvet, brushed cotton and so on.

Material	Distance lorry travelled before stopping
▨	
▨	
▨	

✤ Choose a toy lorry. How far does it go when it is rolled down a slope?

✤ Put some different materials on the floor at the bottom of the slope.

✤ Stick a sample of each material in the box opposite.

✤ Can you find the best way to stop the lorry?

Slippery slopes

Lift the slope.
Metre ruler
Plasticine

* Assemble the slope as shown above.

* Take the wooden block. Place it at the top of the slope.

* Lift the slope slowly until the block slides down.

* In turn, cover the slope with the different materials, such as sugar, sand or plastic sheeting, and observe the effect.

* Which material eases the friction the best? Record your results.

Material	Height when the block slipped
Sugar	
Sand	
Plastic sheeting	
Velvet	

It's a drag!

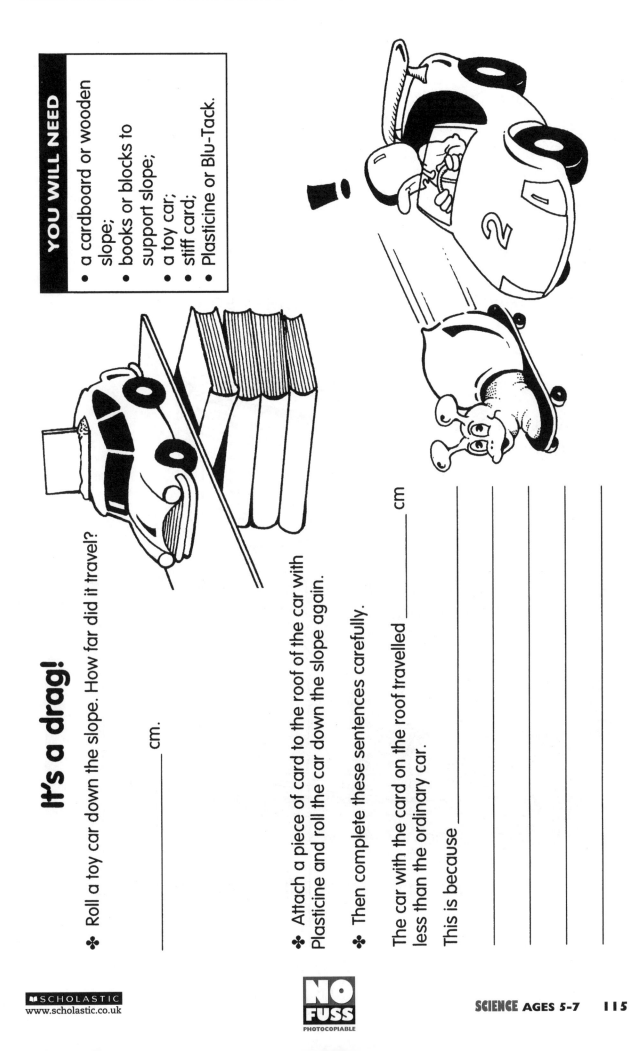

❖ Roll a toy car down the slope. How far did it travel?

_____ cm.

❖ Attach a piece of card to the roof of the car with Plasticine and roll the car down the slope again.

❖ Then complete these sentences carefully.

The car with the card on the roof travelled _____ cm. less than the ordinary car.

This is because _____

_____

_____

_____

YOU WILL NEED

- a cardboard or wooden slope;
- books or blocks to support slope;
- a toy car;
- stiff card;
- Plasticine or Blu-Tack.

Levers – 1

You will need: an empty treacle or paint tin with the lid firmly on; a coin; a screwdriver; a hammer; a nail; a piece of wood.

▲ Try to open the tin using your fingers? Can you do this?

▲ Now try opening the tin using a coin. Is this easier? Why?

▲ Use the screwdriver to open the tin. How easy was this?

The screwdriver acts as a lever to remove the lid. It makes the lid easier to move.

▲ Hammer the nail into the piece of wood, so that half of the nail is still above the wood.

▲ Can you remove the nail with your fingers?

▲ Now use the claw hammer. Why is the hammer easier to use than your fingers?

▲ Make a list of objects that use levers, for example scissors.

■SCHOLASTIC
www.scholastic.co.uk

Levers – 2

You will need: a ruler; a pencil (with flat sides); a 2p coin.

▲ Place the pencil near the edge of the table.

▲ Place the middle of the ruler on top of the pencil.

▲ Put the coin on the ruler near the pencil.

▲ Hit the ruler hard on the end that is off the table. What happens to the coin?

▲ Now move the coin further away from the pencil.
- Hit the ruler again.
- What happens to the coin?
- Has it jumped higher?

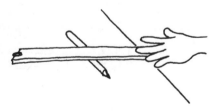

▲ Keep moving the coin along until it is at the end of the ruler. Does the coin jump higher each time?

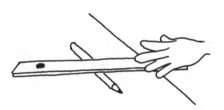

▲ Now move the pencil closer to one end of the ruler and repeat the experiment.
- Does the coin jump higher?
- Can you suggest why?

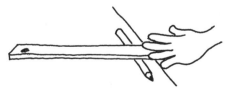

NO FUSS
PHOTOCOPIABLE

See-saw

You will need: a ruler; 2p coins; a pencil (with flat sides).

▲ Place the ruler on the pencil so that it balances. The pencil acts as a pivot (fulcrum).

▲ Place a 2p coin on each end of the ruler until it balances again.

▲ Add another coin to one end. What happens?

▲ Can you now make the ruler balance without adding another coin?

▲ Find out other ways to make the see-saw balance.

Name _____

Make a puppet

You will need: string; paper fasteners; card; scissors; sticky tape; ice lolly stick or dowel.

This puppet uses levers to make it work.

▲ Colour the puppet and cut out the shapes.

▲ Glue the shapes on to card and cut them out.

▲ Join the arms and legs with paper fasteners.

▲ Attach the ice lolly stick to the back using sticky tape.

▲ Join the string to the paper fasteners as shown below.

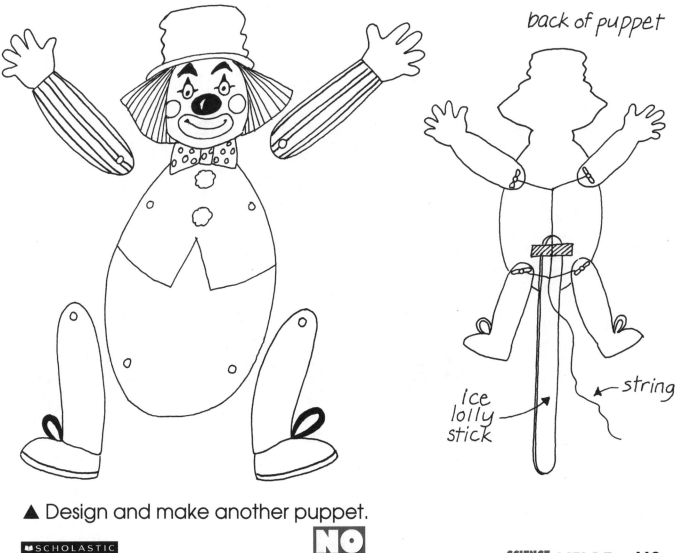

back of puppet

ice lolly stick

string

▲ Design and make another puppet.

Name _____

Where is electricity?

▲ Look at this picture of a classroom. Put an **x** where you would find electricity.

Name _____

Which of these objects use electricity?

▲ Cut out the pictures. Sort them into two groups, ones that use electricity and ones that don't.

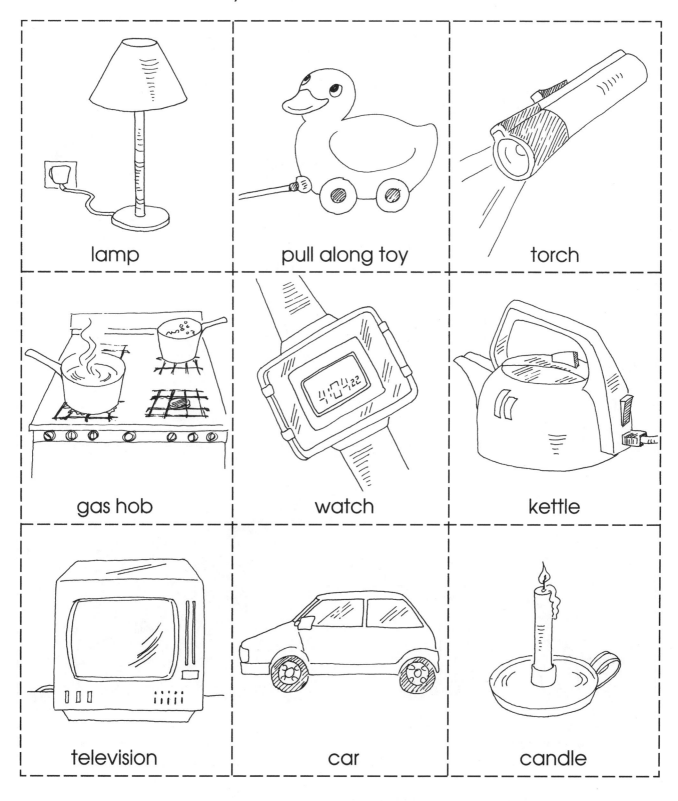

lamp	pull along toy	torch
gas hob	watch	kettle
television	car	candle

▲ Compare your answers with a friend. Do you agree?

What is unsafe here?

▲ Look at these pictures. Put an **x** next to any unsafe object or a person who is doing a dangerous thing.

▲ Share your ideas with your friends.
Do they agree with you?

■ SCHOLASTIC
www.scholastic.co.uk

Name _____

Make a bulb light up

You will need: a 1.5v battery; two pieces of wire; a small bulb; tape to secure wire; a bulb holder; a small screwdriver (optional).

▲ Connect the battery, wires and bulb together so that the bulb lights up. You have made an electrical circuit.

▲ Draw your circuit below.

▲ Draw arrows to show which way you think the electricity is moving.

Which bulb will light up?

▲ Look at the pictures below.
Predict which bulbs will light up.

▲ Try them out to see if you were correct.

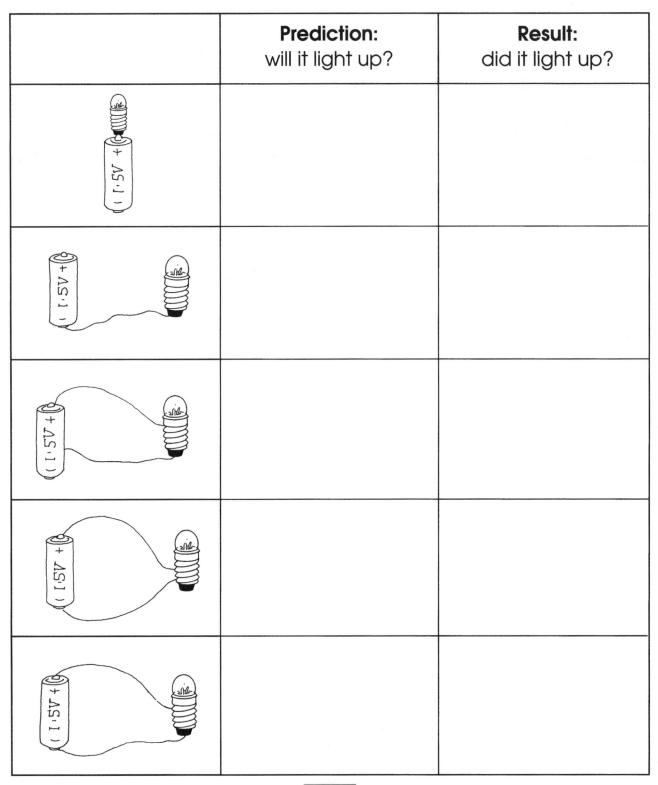

	Prediction: will it light up?	**Result:** did it light up?

Name _____

Make a simple switch

You will need: a 1.5v battery; a small bulb; a bulb holder (or tape); a piece of card (6cm x 6cm); two paper fasteners; two paper-clips.

▲ Make a switch by pushing the paper fasteners through each end of card and attaching paper-clips to the fasteners so that they can touch.

▲ Work out how to attach wires to the battery, bulb and switch so that the light can be turned on and off.

▲ Draw the circuit you made below.

Name _____

Make it buzz!

You will need: 1.5v battery; a buzzer; two
pieces of wire; a box with a lid; paper-clips
or crocodile clips.

▲ Using just the battery and buzzer,
connect the wires of the buzzer to each
end of the battery.
  • Does the buzzer work?
  • Does it work if you swap the wires over?
  • Why do you think this happens?

▲ Make a burglar-alarm jewellery box.
Use the diagrams below to help you.
The box should make a buzzing sound when the lid is lifted.

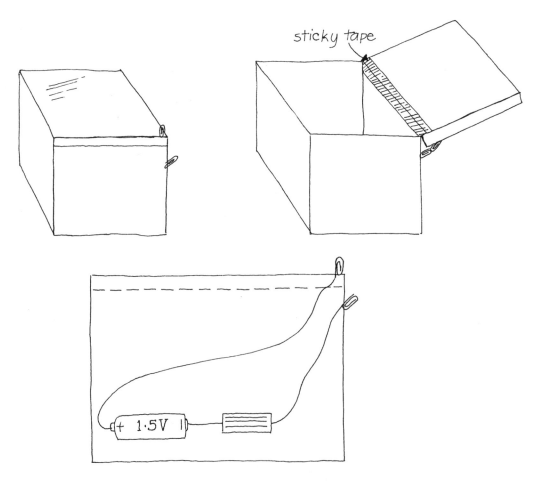

▲ Now try to make a burglar-alarm door.

Will it conduct electricity?

You will need: a 1.5v or 4.5v battery; a bulb and holder; three pieces of wire; two crocodile clips; a number of objects such as teaspoon, wooden ruler, plastic cup, rubber gloves, fabric, fruit and so on.

Some materials will let electricity pass through them (conductors) and others will not (insulators).

▲ Test each object to find out which will conduct electicity. Set up a circuit as shown opposite.

4·5V

▲ Predict which objects will allow electricity to pass through and light the bulb. Now test them.

Object	Prediction: will it conduct?	Result: did it conduct?
metal spoon		
wooden ruler		
plastic cup		
rubber gloves		
woollen cloth		
glass		
silver coin		
piece of fruit		
brass weight		
paper		

In this series:

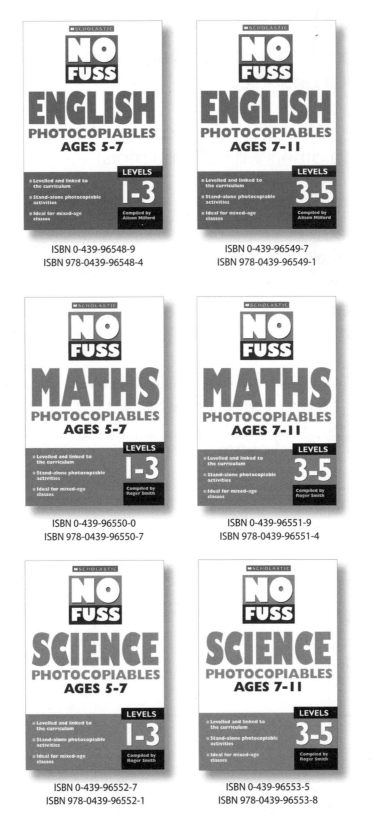

ISBN 0-439-96548-9
ISBN 978-0439-96548-4

ISBN 0-439-96549-7
ISBN 978-0439-96549-1

ISBN 0-439-96550-0
ISBN 978-0439-96550-7

ISBN 0-439-96551-9
ISBN 978-0439-96551-4

ISBN 0-439-96552-7
ISBN 978-0439-96552-1

ISBN 0-439-96553-5
ISBN 978-0439-96553-8

To find out more, call: 0845 603 9091
or visit our website www.scholastic.co.uk